INTRODUCING ISLAMICJERUSALEM

A SERIES OF MONOGRAPHS ON ISLAMICJERUSALEM STUDIES

1. هيثم فتحي الرطروط (2002)، نظرية جديدة لتفسير التصميم والتخطيط الهندسي لقبة الصخرة والفكر التخطيطي الهندسي الإسلامي في الفترة الإسلامية المبكرة، (مجمع البحوث الإسلامية في المملكة المتحدة).

2. Othman Ismael al-Tel (2003), *The first Islamic conquest of Aelia (Islamicjerusalem): A critical analytical study of the early Islamic historical narrations and sources* (Al-Maktoum Institute Academic Press).

3. Aisha Al-Ahlas (2004), *Islamic Research Academy (ISRA): 1994 – 2004 Background, activities and achievements, with special reference to the new field of inquiry of Islamicjerusalem Studies* (Islamic Research Academy).

4. Haithem Fathi Al-Ratrout (2004), *The Architectural development of al-Aqsa Mosque in Islamicjerusalem in the early Islamic period: Sacred architecture in the shape of the 'Holy'* (Al-Maktoum Institute Academic Press).

5. Abd al-Fattah M. El-Awaisi (2005, 2006, 2007), *Introducing Islamicjerusalem* (Al-Maktoum Institute Academic Press).

6. Khalid El-Awaisi (2007), *Mapping Islamicjerusalem: A Rediscovery of Geographical Boundaries* (Al-Maktoum Institute Academic Press).

7. Maher Abu-Munshar (2007), *Islamic Jerusalem and Its Christians: A History of Tolerance and Tensions* (I B Tauris & Co Ltd).

8. Abd al-Fattah El-Awaisi (2007), *Islamicjerusalem Studies: A Guide* (Al-Maktoum Institute Academic Press).

INTRODUCING
ISLAMICJERUSALEM

ABD AL-FATTAH MUHAMMAD EL-AWAISI

Al-Maktoum Institute Academic Press

First published 2005, reprinted 2006 (second edition)
Third edition 2007
Al-Maktoum Institute Academic Press
124 Blackness Road, Dundee DD1 5PE
United Kingdom
Tel: 0044 (0) 1382 908070
Fax: 0044 (0) 1382 908077
www.almipress.com

Monograph on Islamicjerusalem Studies 5

A catalogue record of this book is available from the British Library.
ISBN 978-1-904436-12-6

DEDICATION

- To HH Shaikh Hamdan Bin Rashid Al-Maktoum who gave our contemporary world a practical model for the missing relationship between 'Knowledge and Power' through his continuous support to establish and develop the new field of inquiry of Islamicjerusalem Studies, and to the man who based his vision on the understanding of Islamicjerusalem as a key model for multiculturalism which HH Shaikh Hamdan established on Umar's Assurance of Safety.

- To HE Mr Mirza Hussain Al-Sayegh who has been the key figure in helping to establish the new field of inquiry of Islamicjerusalem Studies, and who made everything possible for this field to develop and flourish.

- To my beloved parents, Muhammad and Sara, who gave me their love and support, showed me the way to success through education, and inculcated me with a love for Islamicjerusalem.

- To my beloved place and concept, Islamicjerusalem.

- To my beloved wife, Aisha, who shared with me every foundation step from which to establish the new field of inquiry of Islamicjerusalem Studies.

- To those individuals, colleagues, and close friends who believe that nothing is impossible, and that dreams can be changed into reality.

- To my partner students who showed their enthusiasm, working as a team, and have been inspired to become part of the next generation of young scholars in Islamicjerusalem Studies.

CONTENTS

INTRODUCTION 1

CHAPTER ONE: ISLAMICJERUSALEM: A NEW CONCEPT AND
DEFINITIONS 7

BACKGROUND 7
DEFINITIONS 9
   I   *Islamicjerusalem* 10
   II *Islamicjerusalem Studies* 14
LATEST RESEARCH ON ISLAMICJERUSALEM STUDIES 17

CHAPTER TWO: THE *BARAKAH* CIRCLE THEORY OF
ISLAMICJERUSALEM 23

MEANING OF THE *BARAKAH*: GROWTH AND EXPANSION 24
THE FIRST CIRCLE: GEOGRAPHICAL LOCATION AND BOUNDARIES OF
ISLAMICJERUSALEM 25
   The Theory 27
   SURROUNDED with, (Hawlahu) 27
THE SECOND CIRCLE: AL-SHAM AND EGYPT 30
THE THIRD CIRCLE TO MAKKAH: FROM *(MIN)*..TO *(ILA)* 31

CHAPTER THREE: THE LAND OF *(AMAL)* HOPE: DISCUSSION
OF THE PROPHET MUHAMMAD'S PLAN FOR
ISLAMICJERUSALEM 37

LAND OF HOPE 37
THE START OF THE CHANGE: PRELIMINARY PRACTICAL STEPS FOR
ISLAMICJERUSALEM IN THE PROPHET'S LIFETIME 42

CHAPTER FOUR: UMAR'S ASSURANCE OF SAFETY *(AMAN)* TO
THE PEOPLE OF AELIA (ISLAMICJERUSALEM): A CRITICAL
ANALYTICAL STUDY OF THE HISTORICAL SOURCES 55

TREATY OR ASSURANCE 57
EARLY ACCOUNTS 58

DISCUSSION OF TIME, PLACE, AND CHAINS OF TRANSMITTERS (ISNADS) OF
THE ASSURANCE VERSIONS 59
DISCUSSION OF AL-TABARI'S VERSION......................................62
  I   Reshaping a new Society and Environment......................................63
  II   Arrangements for Residing in or Leaving Aelia..............................64
  III Exclusion of the Jews from Residing in Aelia................................69
       Date of the Version..76
DISCUSSION OF THE ORTHODOX PATRIARCHATE'S VERSION......................76
  I   External Criticism..78
  II   Internal Criticism..80
CONCLUSION 82

CHAPTER FIVE: ISLAMICJERUSALEM AS A MODEL FOR
CONFLICT RESOLUTION: A MUSLIM THEORETICAL FRAME
OF REFERENCE TOWARDS OTHERS 95

TADAFU' METHODOLOGY..96
CONCEPT OF 'ADL (JUSTICE)..97
THE PRINCIPLE OF NON EXCLUSION 98
CONSTRUCTIVE ARGUMENTATION METHODOLOGY....................................99
OUTCOMES: PEACEFUL CO-EXISTENCE AND MUTUAL RESPECT 100
ISLAMICJERUSALEM AS A MODEL FOR CONFLICT RESOLUTION 102

CHAPTER SIX: ISLAMICJERUSALEM AS A MODEL FOR
MULTICULTURALISM.. 109

THE VISION 110
SHAIKH HAMDAN BIN RASHID AL-MAKTOUM'S VISION FOR
MULTICULTURALISM...122
  United Arab Emirates – Scotland relations....................................124

CHAPTER SEVEN: UNDERSTANDING HISTORICAL ISSUES
RELATED TO ISLAMICJERUSALEM 131

HISTORICAL METHODOLOGY..131
DISCUSSION OF THE CLAIMS OF SOME ORIENTALISTS AND ISRAELI
ACADEMICS..133

CONCLUSION 141

BIBLIOGRAPHY 147

INDEX..159

INTRODUCTION

There has been an urgent need for a book to introduce an intellectually exciting and stimulating new field of inquiry of Islamicjerusalem Studies. Indeed, during the last five years (since 2000), several colleagues and students have been asking the author to prepare such a book. This was felt to be particularly important after the creation of the first chair in Islamicjerusalem Studies, the development of the first and unique taught Master's programme in Islamicjerusalem Studies, and the establishment of the Centre for Islamicjerusalem Studies at Al-Maktoum Institute for Arabic and Islamic Studies in Scotland. Then, the author felt that more time was needed for us to build on the foundations of our understanding of the new terminology for the new concept of Islamicjerusalem, and to create and develop new frame of reference for study it.

Through his teachings and supervisory role, the author has inspired and encouraged his postgraduate students to develop research into this new branch of human knowledge of Islamicjerusalem, its central frame of reference, vital nature, uniqueness, and various other aspects and dimensions. Many of his discussions and arguments, and much of his thought, have been studied seriously by his postgraduate students and developed into essays, dissertations and theses, all of which have contributed very positively to our knowledge of Islamicjerusalem Studies.

His attempts to define Islamicjerusalem and its field of inquiry in the years 2003, 2004 and 2005 encouraged the author to start

2 INTRODUCING ISLAMICJERUSALEM

thinking seriously about writing this book. However, because of his role as Principal and Vice-Chancellor of Al-Maktoum Institute, his main problem was to find an appropriate time to set down his thoughts and arguments on paper. Fortunately, he was able to use his Christmas and New Year vacation to escape from other commitments and start writing. This led to his redoubled efforts to find other opportunities in his busy schedule during 2005 to finish the book.

The book has been written for readers, academic and otherwise, who are interested in understanding Islamicjerusalem and its new field of inquiry. In particular, it provides thorough grounds of knowledge to meet the learning, teaching and research needs of students for scholarly purposes, as well as the needs of those interested in gaining a sound knowledge of Islamicjerusalem. The author claims it to be a significant contribution to, and an essential reference source for, Islamicjerusalem Studies.

It should be noted that this book is not a study of the history or politics of Islamicjerusalem, but a serious and scholarly attempt to explore and introduce Islamicjerusalem and its field aiming to set the scene for advanced research. It is hoped that it will enrich our understanding of this inimitable region, address some of the sensitive, important and key issues on the subject, and open up and promote intellectual and academic debate and understanding of Islamicjerusalem and its role widely enough to shed light on new lines of explanation.

The book is an attempt not only to introduce Islamicjerusalem, but to establish and examine the theoretical and conceptual framework within which to approach the subject. It is hoped it will enable readers to develop their knowledge and understanding of the contemporary academic debates on the nature of Islamicjerusalem, the uniqueness of the Islamicjerusalem region and its effects on the rest of the world in both historical and contemporary contexts, and on the *Barakah* Circle Theory of Islamicjerusalem. Particular attention will be paid to examining the Islamicjerusalem vision and how Muslims have approached Islamicjerusalem. Several questions will be key to this study, such as: Whose is Islamicjerusalem? Can it be shared? Is it an exclusive or inclusive region? What are the reasons for Muslims having close links and concerns with Islamicjerusalem? What is the significance of Islamicjerusalem to Islam and Muslims? Does it have any special status compared with any other regions? How do Muslims respond to the competing claims of other religions?

Accordingly, the aims of this book are to introduce Islamicjerusalem to intellectuals, academics, and the wider public interested in the subject, to identify the nature, identity, characters, and key features of Islamicjerusalem; and to provide a theoretical and conceptual framework for discussion of the role of Islamicjerusalem in historical and contemporary contexts.

Another aim is to lay the intellectual foundations for the new field of inquiry of Islamicjerusalem Studies in scholarship. However, this may be a provocative and challenging issue for those in academic and political establishments who are interested in the region and who may not accept the new field on the basis that it goes beyond their political agenda and attachments, or for those who cannot go along with innovation and new ideas. Indeed, to advance such knowledge, understanding, definitions and approaches is to challenge long-established traditionalist and Orientalist claims.

For a long time, the author was adamant that the political agenda and its activisms and scholarship should be separate. He argues very strongly that political movements, religious or secular, in the Arab Muslim countries restrict the intellectual development of scholars and impose restrictions on their freedom of thought. To be taken seriously, any academic agenda should be taken away from religious or political agendas.

The author has endeavoured, in his interpretations, explanations, analysis and clarification, to concentrate on and look with complete openness at most if not all of the aspects surrounding the issue under discussion, and focus on the key and fundamental ones related to the topic. He has also tried to take a comprehensive, realistic, inclusive and scholarly approach rather than a theological faith stand or one that is politically exclusive. He has adopted the interdisciplinary and multidisciplinary approaches incorporated in the Dundee Declaration for the future development of the Study of Islam and Muslims. Moreover, the author did not embark on his research with a defined theory(ies) of or definition(s) for Islamicjerusalem. Instead, these findings have emerged in the course of his examination and analysis of the data collected systematically throughout the process of this research.

The book depends mainly on Muslim core sources, such as the Qur'an and its commentaries, as well as on books of Prophet Muhammad's traditions, on historical sources and secondary references. Throughout the book, the author has chosen not to depend on any one English translation of the meaning of the Qur'an but to use several English translations. To compare these translations and choose the best, he refers to several of those available including those of: Abdullah Yusuf Ali[1], Muhammad Muhsin Khan and Muhammad Taqi-ud-Din Al-Hilali[2], Muhammad Asad[3], M.A.S. Abdel Haleem[4], and Thomas Cleary[5]. In most cases, he has chosen part of their translation of a particular text adding to it his own translation.

Some available English translations suffered from the translators not understanding the original Arabic texts. To help understand some important Arabic texts and to re-examine the accuracy of these translations, both transliteration and translation were included. Moreover, when translating terminologies from Arabic into English, an attempt has been made by the author to strike a balance between the strength of expression in the original and its exact meaning. However, to avoid the mistranslating of any particular Arabic terminologies, the author employed an approach of not translating these into English but leaving them in their original Arabic language which helps to avoid any leading to different or strange understandings and interpretations.

Within an introduction and a conclusion, the book has been divided into seven chapters. Chapter one introduces the new concept and definitions of Islamicjerusalem and Islamicjerusalem Studies. It also discusses the background of these definitions and highlights the latest research in Islamicjerusalem Studies.

Chapter two presents the *Barakah* Circle Theory of Islamicjerusalem. Particular attention is paid to specific subjects, such as the meaning of *Barakah*, and the geographical location and boundaries of Islamicjerusalem.

Chapter three presents a new terminology, the land of *Amal* (Hope) . It discusses the steps taken by the Prophet and his first successor towards conquering this land. Particular attention is paid to the Prophet's strategic plan which he himself drew up for Islamicjerusalem.

Chapter four presents a critical analytical study of Umar's Assurance of Safety (*Aman)* to the People of Aelia (Islamicjerusalem). It examines and compares most of the available versions of Umar's Assurance. It focuses on the longest and most famous of these, namely the text given by al-Tabari and that published by the Orthodox Patriarchate in Jerusalem in 1953. It also discusses the reasons behind the appearance of various versions of Umar's Assurance.

Chapter five presents Islamicjerusalem as a model for conflict resolution by discussing the Muslim theoretical frame of reference towards others. It also discusses the main key elements of such a model, the methodological approach of *Tadafu'* (counteraction) and the concept of *'Adl* (Justice), the principle of non-exclusion, and the constructive argumentation methodology.

Chapter six presents Islamicjerusalem as a model for multiculturalism. It also highlights Shaikh Hamdan Bin Rashid Al-Maktoum's vision which is based on the understanding of Islamicjerusalem as a model for multiculturalism.

Chapter seven presents an understanding of several historical issues on Islamicjerusalem, and discusses the claims of some Orientalists and Israeli academics on issues related to Islamicjerusalem.

1	Abdullah Yusuf Ali (2003), *The Meaning of the Holy Qur'an* (Islamic Foundation, Leicester).
2	Muhammad Muhsin Khan and Muhammad Taqi-ud-Din Al-Hilali (1996), *Interpretation of the Meaning of the Noble Qur'an* (Dar-us-Salam, Saudi Arabia).
3	Muhammad Asad (2003), *The Message of the Qur'an* (Book Foundation, England).
4	M.A.S. Abdel Haleem (2004), *The Qur'an: a new translation* (Oxford University Press).
5	Thomas Cleary (2004), The Qur'an: a new translation (Starlatch Press, USA).

1

ISLAMICJERUSALEM: A NEW CONCEPT AND DEFINITIONS

As an essential part of introducing Islamicjerusalem, it is important to be clear on what is meant by this new terminology; and a working definition needs to be established. A number of questions need to be raised. Is Islamicjerusalem the same as Jerusalem the city? What sort of Jerusalem are we talking about? Is it simply the area of al-Aqsa Mosque? (This is only one fifth of the Old Walled City.) Is it the Old Walled city of Jerusalem, East Jerusalem, West Jerusalem, Greater Jerusalem, the whole of Palestine or part of Palestine? These all address the question of a definition from a contemporary context. It is important however to link this to a historical context for a definition to be produced.

In addition to introducing new definitions of Islamicjerusalem and Islamicjerusalem Studies, this chapter discusses the background of the new field of inquiry of Islamicjerusalem Studies, and also highlights the latest research on Islamicjerusalem.

Background[1]
The establishment of the new field of inquiry of Islamicjerusalem was a journey that took nearly a decade, 1994-2003, adopting the principle of gradual development and travelling through several stages. It also went through a number of stages on the road to its establishment through an integrated programme which included a number of new academic initiatives and practical steps which include both developing institutional framework and the modes of delivery of the new field.

As part of his vision for the new field, the founder (author) paid particular attention to establishing the concept of Islamicjerusalem Studies in the building of its foundations. From the initial stages he was keen to provide practical steps to deliver the essential contributions of knowledge in the new field to the world of learning, and to encourage young researchers to specialise in this field. These have been delivered mainly through organising an annual international academic conference on Islamicjerusalem Studies (eight to date), the *Journal of Islamicjerusalem Studies*, and the securing of a good number of postgraduate research studentships in Islamicjerusalem Studies. These elements were very significant in creating the new frame of reference for the study of Islamicjerusalem. Indeed, both the annual conference and the *Journal* have successfully 'highlighted the gap in the available literature' on Islamicjerusalem Studies, provided the 'necessary knowledge' to develop the field, and have become an international discussion forum for scholars who are interested in the field[2].

Other serious practical steps were needed to institutionalise the development, integration and promotion of the field. These were initiated by developing the first new unit entitled 'Islamicjerusalem', which the author taught at undergraduate level at the University of Stirling. This unit has been developed into a taught Master's programme at Al-Maktoum Institute. Indeed, to pioneer the field, Al-Maktoum Institute embodied the founder's vision by inaugurating the first and unique taught Master's programme in Islamicjerusalem Studies worldwide. After the establishment of Al-Maktoum Institute came the creation of its first academic post, the first chair in Islamicjerusalem Studies. The Centre for Islamicjerusalem Studies was founded to focus all its efforts, and to play a key role in developing the new field. This was a natural progressive development aimed at structuring the research and teaching of Islamicjerusalem Studies.

Shaikh Hamdan Bin Rashid Al-Maktoum's passion and commitment ensured the development of this new field. In its initial and crucial stage of development, Shaikh Hamdan played an essential part by providing scholarships for young scholars to pursue Islamicjerusalem Studies at postgraduate level. His second major involvement was when he established Al-Maktoum Institute. Aisha al-Ahlas argued that the 'main reason behind the success' of establishing the new field of inquiry of Islamicjerusalem Studies was the 'uniquely close relationship between the two elements, knowledge and power.'[3] This formal model of relationship between ruler and scholar is absent in Arab and Muslim countries. Indeed, as stated in the *Dundee Declaration for the Future Development of the Study of Islam and Muslims* on 18 March 2004, one of 'the crises in the contemporary Muslim world is the absence of co-operation between knowledge and power.'

Definitions

In the first few years of establishing the new field, a number of Arab and Muslim scholars were very concerned about this new terminology, especially the word 'Islamic'. Their main worry was that the use of this word could open up hostility and non-acceptance by some Western scholars. At that time, the author's main counter-argument was that, without the term Islamic, the whole terminology would lose its niche, meaning and definition. In addition, if it were to be only Jerusalem without the term Islamic, which Jerusalem would we be talking about? There were also already many research and teaching programmes in Jerusalem Studies which meant that our contribution to knowledge would be very limited. However, Islamicjerusalem opened up a new area of specialisation with a new frame of reference. Probably the term Islamic could be the right term to shock, cover new ground, promote serious dialogue and initiate debates that may shed light on new lines of explanation and new horisons of critical thinking.

After the initial research on Umar's Assurance of Safety to the people of Aelia, the author started from 2000 to develop his new findings. In 2004 this helped to define both Islamicjerusalem and Islamicjerusalem Studies. Indeed, Umar's Assurance was the jewel of the first Muslim *Fatih* (i.e., introducing new stage and vision) of Aelia, and the beacon for developing Islamicjerusalem's unique and creative vision and nature.

I Islamicjerusalem

Aisha al-Ahlas argued that the fifth international academic conference on Islamicjerusalem Studies held on 21 April 2003 was 'a turning point' in the history of the new field of inquiry of Islamicjerusalem Studies[4]. Although he was the one who in 1994 had invented this new terminology of Islamicjerusalem, a coherent definition was not possible when the author was trying, especially in the last five years (2000 – 2005), to come to an understanding of what he specifically meant by Islamicjerusalem. This is due to the complex nature of the concept.

On 21 April 2003 in the fifth international academic conference on Islamicjerusalem 'Islamicjerusalem: Prophetic Temples and al-Aqsa Mosque Demystifying Realities and Exploring Identities', the author presented a keynote speech on 'Exploring the identity of Islamicjerusalem'. Here he publicly admitted that 'It took me nearly three years to come to the working definition which I would like to present to you today". He added 'We need to start with a working definition. So, what do we mean by Islamicjerusalem? …'.

Although the author did not at that time present his final definition of Islamicjerusalem, his presentation contained the key elements: 'There are three elements of this working definition. Its geographical location (land), its people (i.e.: who live or used to live there) and its vision to administer or to rule that land and its people. It is not possible to separate these three elements as they are interlinked. In addition, they are linked with their historical context.' (For the author, if geography is the theatre, history is the play) For the first time, he argued that Islamicjerusalem is not a mere city or another urban settlement, but a region which includes several cities, towns and villages. From this definition, it can be seen that Islamicjerusalem is to be described as a region with three key interlinked elements. Identifying the centre of the *Barakah* led him to develop a new significant innovative theory, 'the *Barakah* Circle Theory of Islamicjerusalem.' As is discussed in chapter two, this theory is based on new interpretations of the core Muslim sources and history. He also made the same point when he presented his public lecture at the Academy of Islamic Studies at the University of Malaya on 24 September 2004. However, what is presented here is the revised definition which takes into consideration the discussions the author has had since then, and the new definition of Islamicjerusalem Studies.

Islamicjerusalem is a new terminology for a new concept, which may be translated into the Arabic language as *Bayt al-Maqdis*. It can be fairly and eventually characterised and defined as a unique region laden with a rich historical background, religious significances, cultural attachments, competing political and religious claims, international interests and various aspects that affect the rest of the world in both historical and contemporary contexts. It has a central frame of reference and a vital nature with three principal intertwined elements: its geographical location (land and boundaries), its people (population), and its unique and creative inclusive vision, to administer that land and its people, as a model for multiculturalism[5].

The term *Bayt al-Maqdis* has been used in the past in both core and early Muslim narratives and sources to refer to the Aelia region.[6] It may be claimed that Prophet Muhammad was the first to use the term *Bayt al-Maqdis* to refer to that region. Indeed he used both terms, Aelia and *Bayt al-Maqdis*, in many of his traditions. However, one can argue that the Arabs before the advent of Islam may also have used the same term to refer to the same region. Although the Prophet did use *Bayt al-Maqdis*, the author cannot be certain who was the first to use the term[7].

The word-for-word translation of the Arabic term *Bayt al-Maqdis* could be 'the Holy House'. This might be understood from a theological point of view, but it would definitely be difficult to understand from historical and geographical contexts. In addition, the use of the term *Bayt al-Maqdis* does not represent the definition which has been presented in this section. This is especially true after it became obvious that Islamicjerusalem is a new concept which carries historical, geographical, religious, cultural, and political backgrounds. In addition, it is also not only al-Aqsa Mosque nor the Walled City of Jerusalem, as some outdated arguments might suggest. Indeed, it is not just a city nor yet another urban settlement, but a region which includes several villages, towns, and cities which has an inclusive multicultural vision. In short, the new terminology of Islamicjerusalem cannot be understood without placing it in historical, geographical and religious contexts.

However, the terminology Islamicjerusalem was a new concept which appeared and was used in its comprehensive sense for the first time originally in the English language by this author, as has been documented, characterised and defined in this chapter. It should be noted that Islamicjerusalem is one word not two separate words, i.e. Islamic and Jerusalem. It should also be made clear that Islamicjerusalem is not the same as Jerusalem or Islamic Quds *al-Quds al-Islamiyyah*. It is also different from Muslim Jerusalem as in Jewish Jerusalem and Christian Jerusalem. The historical period when the Muslims ruled Islamicjerusalem for several centuries should be called Muslim Jerusalem and not Islamicjerusalem. Islamicjerusalem is a new concept, whereas Muslim Jerusalem refers to the periods when Muslims ruled Islamicjerusalem. To illustrate this point, Umar Ibn al-Khattab's *Fatih* of the region is the first Muslim *Fatih* of Islamicjerusalem. Indeed, this should also apply to the later Muslim period up to 1917 and to any Muslim rule of Islamicjerusalem in the future. In addition, contemporary Muslim Jerusalem is shaped in part by dialogue with the concept of Islamicjerusalem, the classical and modern history of Muslims, and in part by response to external interests and influences in the region. Accordingly, contemporary Muslims seek to relate their heritage in Muslim Jerusalem from the concept of Islamicjerusalem and the Muslim past to the radical situation of today.

It is worth mentioning that, since its launch in the winter of 1997, the *Journal of Islamicjerusalem Studies* has also carried the Arabic term *Al-Quds al-Islamiyyah* or Islamic Quds. However, the author's new findings on Umar's Assurance of Safety to the people of Aelia have led to a change in the use of that Arabic term. The change of the Arabic title of the *Journal of Islamicjerusalem Studies* from *Al-Quds al-Islamiyyah* to Bayt al-Maqdis occurred in the summer 2000 issue. This was the same issue of the *Journal* which published the author's article on Umar's Assurance in both the English and Arabic languages.

The last part of the definition has been partly borrowed from the political science theory of the three elements of any state, but replaces the concept of sovereignty with the vision of inclusivity and plurality of Islamicjerusalem. Indeed, this unique creative vision of Islamicjerusalem is more important than the issue of sovereignty in the case of Islamicjerusalem. It could be argued that the final product is normally the issue of sovereignty. However, the agenda for Islamicjerusalem should not be the desire to achieve colonial goals of ruling lands and people which could be based either on economic ambitions or on racist nationalist and theological claims, or on any other interests and claims. If there is no vision, or a vision of exclusivity, in Islamicjerusalem, sovereignty would naturally lead internally to oppression, divisions in society and its communities, and externally to the involvement of external powers to try to resolve these internal troubles and problems, which would lead to instability and barriers to the steady progress and prosperity of the region. Indeed, the unique aspect of Islamicjerusalem is highlighted through its vision, which presents a model for peaceful co-existence and a way for people from different religious and cultural backgrounds to live together in an environment of multiculturalism and religious and cultural engagement, diversity and tolerance.

This understanding of Islamicjerusalem as a model for multiculturalism was presented by the author, for the first time, in his public lecture on 'Islamicjerusalem as a Model for Multiculturalism' at the Academy of Islamic Studies at the University of Malaya on 24 September 2004. It was based on the findings of his research on Umar's Assurance in 2000. However, in this book is the revised presentation, which takes into consideration the discussions the author has had since then, especially the revised version of Umar's Assurance in this book, and the new definitions of Islamicjerusalem and Islamicjerusalem Studies.

II   Islamicjerusalem Studies

The sixth international academic conference on Islamicjerusalem Studies organised on 31 May 2004 celebrated the tenth anniversary of the foundation of the new field of inquiry of Islamicjerusalem Studies. This was another significant event in the history of the new field. Indeed, in his keynote speech, the founder presented for the first time his definition of Islamicjerusalem Studies. However, what is presented here is the revised definition of Islamicjerusalem Studies, which has taken into consideration more recent discussions and the new definition of Islamicjerusalem.

> **Islamicjerusalem Studies** can be fairly eventually characterised and defined as a new branch of human knowledge based on interdisciplinary and multidisciplinary approaches. It aims to investigate all matters related to the Islamicjerusalem region, explore and examine its various aspects, and provide a critical analytic understanding of the new frame of reference, in order to identify the nature of Islamicjerusalem and to understand the uniqueness of this region and its effects on the rest of the world in both historical and contemporary contexts.

Indeed, Islamicjerusalem Studies is a field of inquiry which covers several disciplines, such as the study of Islam and Muslims, history and archaeology, art and architecture, geography and geology, environment and politics, and other related disciplines. Accordingly, it has interdisciplinary and multidisciplinary approaches which include historical and theological, theoretical and conceptual, empirical and cultural approaches. The new field also adopts the policy of escaping the trap of reacting to others and trying to engage with them through creating a new agenda, dialogue and debate on the subject which will lead to more constructive dialogue between scholars in several disciplines.

The new field will not only provide an understanding of Islamicjerusalem but will examine the new frame of reference within which Muslims approach Islamicjerusalem. Several questions will be key to addressing this point: What are the reasons for Muslims having close links to and concern with Islamicjerusalem? What is the significance of Islamicjerusalem to Islam and to Muslims? Does Islamicjerusalem have any special status compared with any other region?

In-depth discussion of the various aspects and dimensions of Islamicjerusalem will open up new horizons for those interested in understanding its vision, nature and the reasons for its distinctness from other regions. For example, the study of the inclusive vision of Islamicjerusalem should not only be restricted to its people's religions and cultures, it should also include 'equal measures' of the roles of its two genders, male and female. A young promising Egyptian scholar, Sarah Hassan, argues that:

> Women as much as men left their marks in the beginning of the Muslim history of, and the physical attachment to, Islamicjerusalem, and both genders played a role in asserting its inclusiveness to religions and genders. [Only] when this crucial element of inclusiveness is sufficiently taken into account, can Islamicjerusalem become a model for 'multiculturalism' in practice.[8]

As 'gender' has become 'a useful category of historical analysing',[9] the author agrees with Sarah Hassan's argument that 'the usage of gender as a tool of analysing both its (Islamicjerusalem) past and present is a necessity for the completion and advancement of this new field of inquiry (of Islamicjerusalem Studies).'[10]

In order to demonstrate this inclusive vision, there is a need to use gender as a tool of analysis in approaching the study of Islamicjerusalem through examining the active role played by Muslim women and their vital contributions in underpinning and demonstrating the significance of Islamicjerusalem. This calls for a re-examination of the interpretation of the Qur'anic verses, the Ahadith that were narrated, and the Muslim juristical rulings that were made by Muslim women and compare them with those made by Muslim men regarding Islamicjerusalem. Also Muslim women's participation should be compared and their role reinstated in the making of Islamicjerusalem history in all its periods. For example, Sarah Hassan claims of the Mother of Believers, Safiyyah Bint Huyayyi Ibn Akhtab that her 'life story in general, and her visit to Islamicjerusalem in particular, illustrate vividly, how the whole process of negotiating her Jewish background and her Muslim religion culminates in Islamicjerusalem.'[11]

In addition, this new field could be argued as consolidating the Qur'anic, Hadith and Muslim historical disciplines by shedding light on new lines of explanation. Numerous verses revealed about Islamicjerusalem in the Qur'an, and about the frequency with which the Prophet spoke about Islamicjerusalem[12], lead one to argue that the new field has revealed greater insights into several disciplines such as the interpretation of the Qur'an and the Ahadith. In addition, it has clarified several contradicting historical events and resolved a number of problematic historical issues.

Finally, one could argue that a definition should be short, precise and to the point, yet these definitions of Islamicjerusalem are very long. However, what has been provided for the first time is a scholarly presentation of what can be fairly eventually characterised and defined of Islamicjerusalem and its field. So the definition is not only the definition but also the characteristics of these definitions. Moreover, these definitions which appear for the first time in this format try to shock, confuse, and throw doubt on some of what has been taken for granted in the past by scholars representing various schools of thought, trends, and approaches. Such definitions also aim to raise questions and provide researchers and scholars in the field with the key aspects of Islamicjerusalem.

Although these definitions are the author's most important contributions to the field, they should be considered as working definitions, to set the scene for the field's future development. They by no means claim to be theological or divinity *Ilahiyyat* definitions which cannot be changed or developed, as some Muslim traditionalist theologians would claim. They are, as in the case of Islamicjerusalem Studies, characterised and defined as a new 'branch of human knowledge'. Indeed, there are human explanations and interpretations of new concepts and terminology which are continually subject to change and development based on the latest scholarly research in the field.

Latest Research on Islamicjerusalem Studies

Al-Maktoum Institute has developed unique teaching programmes, based on current and progressive research, which take into consideration the needs and preferences of our local, national and international students, so that they can appreciate and understand the various schools of thought within a specific line of study. This has produced waves of postgraduate students with a first Master's degree in Islamicjerusalem Studies[13], students who hopefully now have a thorough grounding in the new field.

In addition, the Institute has trained qualified students and created a team of young scholars in a variety of disciplines in Islamicjerusalem Studies and has conducted high quality research either at taught Master or PhD levels. For example, the following list contains some of the latest research on Islamicjerusalem Studies:

1. Othman Ismael al-Tel wrote his PhD thesis (2002) on *The first Islamic conquest of Aelia (Islamicjerusalem): A critical analytical study of the early Islamic historical narrations and sources.* (July 2003)
2. Haithem Fathi Al-Ratrout wrote his PhD thesis (2002) on *The architectural development of Al-Aqsa Mosque in Islamicjerusalem in the early Islamic period: Sacred architecture in the shape of the 'Holy'.*
3. Maher Younes Abu-Munshar wrote his PhD thesis (2003) on *A historical study of Muslim treatment of Christians in Islamicjerusalem at the time of Umar Ibn al-Khattab and Salah al-Din with special reference to the Islamic values of justice.* (Nov 2003)

4. Mohammad Roslan Mohammad Nor wrote his PhD thesis on *The significance of Islamicjerusalem in Islam: Qur'anic and Hadith perspectives*. (Dec 2005)

5. Aminurraasyid Yatiban wrote his Master's dissertation (2003) on *The Islamic concept of sovereignty: Islamicjerusalem during the first Islamic conquest as a case study*. He also wrote his PhD thesis on *Muslim understandings of the concept of Al-Siyada (sovereignty): an analytical study of Islamicjerusalem from the first Muslim conquest until the end of the first Abasid period (16-264AH/637-877CE)* (April 2006).

6. Khalid Abd al-Fattah El-Awaisi wrote his Master's dissertation (2003) on *Mapping Islamicjerusalem: Geographical boundaries of Islamicjerusalem*. He also wrote his PhD thesis on *The geographical extent of the land of Bayt al-Maqdis, the Holy Land and the Land of Barakah* (Aug 2006)

7. Ra'id Jabareen wrote his PhD thesis on *Muslim juristic rulings of Islamicjerusalem with special reference to Ibadat in Al-Aqsa Mosque: A critical comparative study* (April 2006).

8. Fatimatuzzahra' Abd Rahman wrote her Master's dissertation (2004) on *Political, social and religious changes in Islamicjerusalem from the first Islamic conquest until the end of Umayyad period (637 to 750CE): An analytical study*. She is now writing her PhD thesis on *The Muslim concept of change: An analytical study of the political, social and economic changes in Islamicjerusalem from the first Muslim conquest till the end of the Fatimid period (637-1099 CE)*.

9. Abdallah Ma'rouf Omar wrote his Master's dissertation (2005) on *Towards the conquest of Islamicjerusalem: the three main practical steps taken by Prophet Muhammad – Analytical study*. He is now writing his PhD thesis on *The Prophet plan towards Islamicjerusalem*.

10. Mahmoud Mataz Kazmouz wrote his Master's dissertation (2006) on *The Ottoman implementation of the vision of Islamicjerusalem as a model for multiculturalism with a special reference to Sultan Suleiman I, the magnificent (1520 – 1566)*. He is now writing his PhD thesis on *Islamicjerusalem as a model for multiculturalism*.

11. Aisha Muhammad Ibrahim Al-Ahlas wrote her Master's dissertation (2003) on *Islamic Research Academy (ISRA) 1994-2003: background, activities and achievements with special reference to the new field of inquiry of Islamic Jerusalem Studies.*

12. Sarah Mohamed Sherif Abdel-Aziz Hassan wrote her Master's dissertation (2005) on *Women: active agents in Islamising[14] Islamicjerusalem from the Prophet's time until the end of the Umayyed period.*

13. Ramona Ahmed Ibrahim wrote her Master's dissertation (2005) on *Islamicjerusalem as a model of conflict resolution: a case study of the negotiations between Salah al-Din and Richard the Lionheart (1191 – 1192 CE).*

In short, with determination and clear vision the new field of inquiry of Islamicjerusalem Studies was founded, together with interdisciplinary and multidisciplinary approaches, and a new frame of reference on Islamicjerusalem was established. Through the establishment of the Academy, the founder (author) planned that research and scholarship take place in building the foundation stones of his vision for the field. In addition, through taking practical steps, he institutionalised the development, integration and promotion of the new field within academia, especially within the British higher education establishments.

---

1   This background of the new field of inquiry of Islamicjerusalem Studies was based on Aisha al-Ahlas (2004), *Islamic Research Academy: 1994-2004, background, activities and achievements, with special reference to the new field of inquiry of Islamicjerusalem Studies* (ISRA, Scotland).

2   Ibid., p. 35.

3   Ibid., p. 80.

4   Ibid., p. 32.

5   According to the Oxford English Dictionary, terminology means a 'set of terms relating to a subject'; term (s) means 'a word or phrase used to describe a thing or to express an idea'; concept means 'an abstract idea'; abstract means 'having to do with ideas or qualities rather than physical or concrete things'; nature means 'the typical qualities or character of a person, animal, or thing'; and vital means

'absolutely necessary'. The author is very grateful to Sarah Hassan, an MLitt postgraduate student in Islamicjerusalem Studies, for collecting these definitions from the Oxford English Dictionary.

6 Othman Ismael Al-Tel (2003), *The first Islamic conquest of Aelia (Islamicjerusalem): A critical analytical study of the early Islamic historical narrations and sources* (Al-Maktoum Institute Academic Press, Scotland), p. 291.

7 The use of this terminology *Bayt al-Maqdis* needs further research.

8 Sarah Mohamed Sherif Abdel-Aziz Hassan (2005), *Women: Active Agents in Islamising Islamicjerusalem from the Prophet's Time until the End of the Umayyed Period,* (Unpublished Master's dissertation, Al-Maktoum Institute for Arabic and Islamic Studies), p. 69.

9 Joan Wallach Scott (1999), *Gender and the Politics of History*, (Columbia University Press, New York), pp. 28-50.

10 Sarah Mohamed Sherif Abdel-Aziz Hassan (2005), *Women: Active Agents in Islamising Islamicjerusalem from the Prophet's Time until the End of the Umayyed Period,* pp 2-3.

11 Ibid., p. 54. In the conclusion, Sarah Hassan presented her dissertation as 'merely the cornerstone for a whole range of possible further gender studies on Islamicjerusalem. The interdisciplinary and multidisciplinary approaches that characterise Islamicjerusalem Studies must be utilised in further discussions and examinations of gender in Islamicjerusalem.' p. 69.

12 Abd al-Fattah El-Awaisi (1998), 'The significance of Jerusalem in Islam: an Islamic reference', *Journal of Islamicjerusalem Studies,* vol. 1, no. 2 (Summer 1998), p. 49.

13 The total number to date is twenty-two. Among them, five have registered for their PhD degree in Islamicjerusalem Studies. During this coming academic year, 2005/2006, four more postgraduate students will begin the taught Master's in Islamicjerusalem Studies.

14 The author strongly disagrees with the usage of this terminology, 'Islamising Islamicjerusalem', in the context of Sarah's dissertation. Indeed, it goes against the recent historical findings, the historical nature of Islamicjerusalem, and its vision at the time under discussion in her dissertation. After she submitted her dissertation, the author felt bound to discuss this issue with Sarah at length. He also raised the point that, on examination of the dissertation, it was revealed that she did not mean 'Islamising Islamicjerusalem'. In addition, he pointed out that she used phrases such as 'underpinning the significance of Islamicjerusalem', 'demonstrating

the significance of Islamicjerusalem', 'making the significance of Islamicjerusalem', and 'developing the significance of Islamicjerusalem'. Sarah agrees that this is not the appropriate terminology to use in this context.

2

THE *BARAKAH* CIRCLE THEORY OF ISLAMICJERUSALEM

The most comprehensive Qur'anic terminology which encompasses Islamicjerusalem's virtues and special features is the land of *Barakah*. Islamicjerusalem is mentioned as the land of the *Barakah* five times in four chapters in the Qur'an, all of which were revealed in Makkah (Qur'an, 21:71, 21:81, 34:18, 7:137, and 17:1). The first four verses which relate to the period before the rise of Islam refer to it as, '*Al-Ard al-lati Barakna fiha*', the land which 'we have given *Barakah*'. The fifth verse which is associated with the Night Journey of Prophet Muhammad refers to al-Aqsa Mosque, *Al-ladhi Barakna Hawlahu,* which 'we have surrounded with *Barakah*'.

This means that the four first verses refer to the whole land which has been given *Barakah,* which could be defined geographically with boundaries, while the fifth refers to the central point of the land which was surrounded with *Barakah*, which would be difficult if not impossible to define geographically. In short, one can argue that the first four verses refer to the region of Islamicjerusalem, while the fifth refers to the centre of the *Barakah* in Islamicjerusalem, al-Aqsa Mosque. However, according to one verse in the Qur'an, the *Barakah* is in the Ka'bah in Makkah, 'the first house [of worship] ever established for people was that at Bakkah (Makkah), a house of *Barakah*', *Mubarakan* (Qur'an, 3:96). Accordingly, the *Barakah* is in the Ka'bah while, in Islamicjerusalem, the *Barakah* surrounds al-Aqsa Mosque.

Identifying the centre of the *Barakah* led the author to develop a new theory called the *Barakah* Circle theory of Islamicjerusalem. This is based on a new interpretation of the core Muslim sources and history. The main aim of this chapter is to present this new theory. Particular attention will be paid to specific subjects, such as the meaning of *Barakah*, and the geographical location and boundaries of Islamicjerusalem.

Meaning of the *Barakah*: Growth and expansion

Although one could argue that *Barakah* is a divine goodness placed in a thing, the author found it very difficult to translate this concept of *Barakah* into the English language. The meaning of the *Barakah*, in the light of the first verse of chapter 17 and other Qur'anic verses and Prophetic traditions, could be defined as growth and expansion. Muslim scholars in general and scholars of *Tafsir* in particular have discussed the manifestations of *Barakah* but not its reality. Although the *Barakah* is invisible, its effects are visible since we can witness its manifestations.

One can divide the manifestations of *Barakah* into two distinguishable types, physical and spiritual. The physical material *Barakah*, for example, manifested itself in Islamicjerusalem's exceptional strategic geographical location and its various material features, which include several topographical locations and climates, and a variety of its agricultural products. The spiritual *Barakah* is represented mainly in the fact that for Jews, Christians and Muslims it is the Prophets' land[1]. In short, one can feel and see these manifested elements of the *Barakah* everywhere in Islamicjerusalem and in its surrounding areas.

If Makkah's and Madinah's *Barakah* are exclusive to Muslims, Islamicjerusalem's *Barakah* is for everyone in the universe. According to one verse in the Qur'an, Islamicjerusalem is 'the land which We have given *Barakah* **for everyone in the universe'** (Qur'an 21:71). As this verse relates to the time of Prophet Abraham, one can argue that this global *Barakah* in Islamicjerusalem was given to it before the period of Prophet

Abraham, if not since the creation of the world. Indeed, the uniqueness of Islamicjerusalem is that the *Barakah* had been given to it well before it became the land of the Prophets. Being the Prophets' land is only one part of the manifestation of this *Barakah*. This global common space of openness and *Barakah* made Islamicjerusalem an ideal destination region for everyone to live there and enjoy this *Barakah*.

The First Circle: Geographical Location and Boundaries of Islamicjerusalem

The first element is to establish and define the boundaries of Islamicjerusalem[2]. The author's hypothesis is that, from historical and geographical points of view, Islamicjerusalem is not just a small or mere city surrounded by walls or another urban settlement, but a region which includes several towns, cities and villages. A young scholar, Khalid El-Awaisi, who has written his PhD thesis on the geographical boundaries of Islamicjerusalem, successfully presented several pieces of evidence to support and demonstrate this hypothesis[3]. One of these pieces of evidence, for example, is the statement made by the first Muslim Caliph, Abu Bakr, when he divided leaders of the army and allocated to them specific regions in historical Syria. According to a unique account, mentioned solely by Al-Waqidi, Abu Bakr explicitly told Amr Ibn Al-Aas that he was assigned to 'Palestine and Aelia', *Alayka bi Filistin wa Illia*[4]. In the Arabic language, the 'wa' which means 'and' could also mean disconnection and distinction between two different things. Here it means two separate regions or that the second region mentioned after the 'wa' is more significant or more important or that more emphasis has been placed on the second region.

Later on, when the second Muslim Caliph, Umar Ibn Khattab, conquered Aelia, he used in his historic document known as Umar's Assurance of Safety the terminology which was well known to the people at that time: 'Aelia'. The Muslims did not change its name immediately. They used it up to the early times of the Umayyads when there existed coins of that name. As is discussed in chapter four, it was the practice of the Rashidun (the first four Caliphs) when conquering a region to simply endorse already existing arrangements and not to introduce major changes.

Several prominent classical Muslim scholars have defined the geographical boundaries of Islamicjerusalem. Without going into much detail about the differences between them in measurements, the author adopts the latest findings of Khalid El-Awaisi[5] on this issue. He concludes by arguing that Islamicjerusalem, as mentioned by classical Muslim scholars, was about 40 miles by 40 miles.

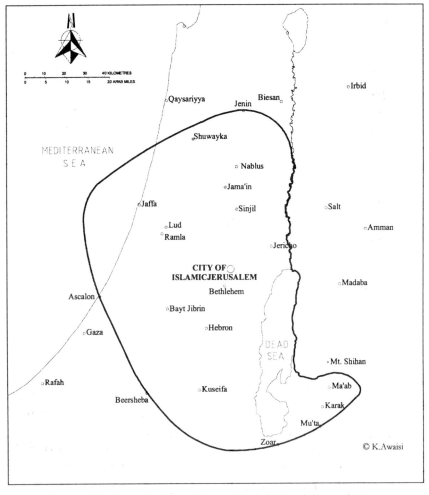

Map 1: The boundaries of the region of Islamicjerusalem

Even in the late Ottoman period, during the rule of the Caliph Abdul Hamid II, we find similar administration boundaries with a slightly different variation. In 1887 this region was known as 'the Excellent Independent Province of Jerusalem', *Liwa' al-Quds al-Mustaqil al-Mumtaz*. It was linked directly with Istanbul and included the following provinces: Jerusalem, Jaffa, Hebron, Gaza, and Beersheba[6]. In short, Islamicjerusalem is not a city or another urban settlement, but a region which includes several villages, towns, and cities, of which al-Aqsa Mosque is the centre.

The Theory

The author would like to borrow the terminology of the Circle Theory, a well-known theory in political science, and would like to adapt it to his understanding of a very significant verse in the Qur'an which emphasises the concept of the *Barakah*. The celebrated fifteenth-century scholar, al-Suyuti, argues that 'if there is only that verse in chapter 17:1 on the significance of Islamicjerusalem it will be indeed enough and includes all kinds of *Barakah*.' The author focuses on this verse mentioning *Barakah*:

> Glory to He Who did take His worshipper, Muhammad, for a journey by night **from** Al-Haram Mosque [at Makkah] **to** al-Aqsa Mosque [at Islamicjerusalem], which we have **surrounded** with *Barakah, Al-ladhi Barakna Hawlahu.* (Qur'an, 17:1)

SURROUNDED with (Hawlahu)

For the purpose of this chapter, the author first focuses on the word *Hawlahu,* **(surrounded)**. Firstly, though the author would like to state that he disagrees with the common scholarly mistranslation of the meaning of this verse of the Qur'an as 'neighbourhood' (e.g. Muhammad Muhsin Khan and Muhammad Tariq-ud-Din Al-Hilali) or 'precincts' (e.g. abdullah Yusuf Ali; and Thomas Cleary). The author argues that the correct translation of *Hawlahu* is a more dynamic and less fixed 'around' or 'surrounding it.'

It may be interesting to note that the Qur'an has thirty parts and chapter 17 is placed as the last chapter of the middle of the Qur'an. Indeed, this chapter starts with the beginning of part fifteen, and ends the first half of the Qur'an. Moreover, the first verse at the ending of the first half of the Qur'an is the verse related to the argument under discussion. It is fortunate that the verse which advances the development of the *Barakah* Circle Theory of Islamicjerusalem is a central verse in the Qur'an. The author was overwhelmed with this finding, as it strengthens his theory. It also responds to the Orientalists who generally underestimate the relevance of the Qur'an to the thinking of Muslims, and particularly the importance of Islamicjerusalem within the Qur'an.

According to this verse, the centre of the *Barakah* is in al-Aqsa Mosque, which means that al-Aqsa Mosque is the place where the origin of *Barakah* is central. In addition, the *Barakah* moves in circles around that Mosque, which might be difficult to measure. This led the author to argue that *Barakah* reached all parts of the world, though not on the same scale. This means that, if you are living near to the centre, you are very close to the epicentre of the *Barakah*. If you live further away from the centre, you will have some *Barakah* but not to the same level of someone living in the centre. In other words, the *Barakah, which travels in circles around al-Aqsa Mosque,* is gradually diminished the further you move away from the centre. Indeed, the Mosque is the centre of the *Barakah* and the rest of the world receives the *Barakah*'s radiation in circles from there. In short, the centre of the *Barakah* is in al-Aqsa Mosque and the *Barakah* moves in circles around that Mosque.

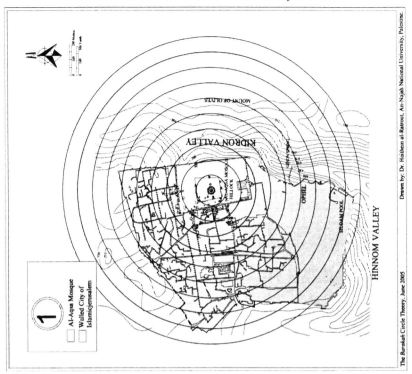

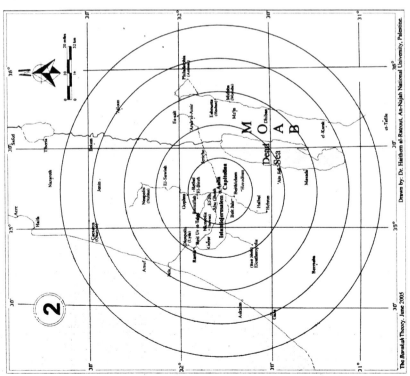

The Second Circle: Al-Sham and Egypt

Most of the traditional Muslim scholars who have interpreted the verse and related it to some traditions of Muhammad suggest that *Al-Ardh al-Mubaraka*, (the *Mubarakah* Land), is related to al-Sham, historical Syria (lies to the north and north east of Islamicjerusalem). However, as the *Barakah* is flowing in circles around the whole area of Islamicjerusalem, these Muslim scholars have restricted the *Barakah* to al-Sham, which is only half of the circle. Why did these scholars ignore the other half of the circle lying to the south? This in itself needs a full research and is beyond the current research. However, according to this theory, *Al-Ardh al-Mubaraka* is not only al-Sham or Egypt but both of them together.

The author argues that ignoring this Qur'anic fact has led to the loss of Islamicjerusalem to foreign powers several times in history. However, when the Muslims at the time of Salah al-Din realised the unity of the two parts of the circle, they liberated Islamicjerusalem from foreign invasion. Indeed, the uniting of Egypt with Syria was an important factor in liberating Islamicjerusalem. Accordingly, the liberation of Islamicjerusalem, one could argue, will not happen until Muslims realise and implement the unity of the two sides in the circle.

There is an obvious link between three distinctive places on earth: Islamicjerusalem, Sinai and Makkah. 'By the figs and the olives [in Islamicjerusalem], and Mount Sinai, and this secure land [in Makkah]' (Qur'an, 95:1-3). Indeed, one can argue that there is a unity between al-Sham and Egypt, with its centre in Islamicjerusalem, and the Arabian Peninsula, with its centre in Makkah and extending between the Nile and the Euphrates.

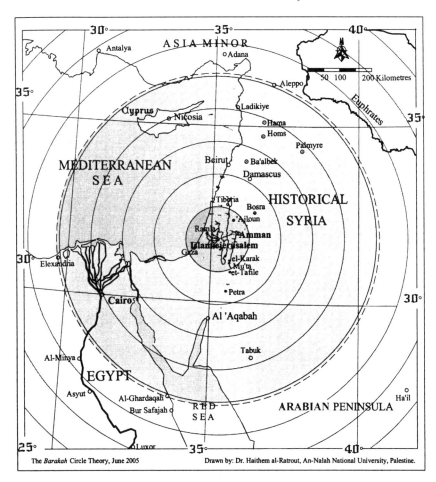

The *Barakah* Circle Theory, June 2005   Drawn by: Dr. Haithem al-Ratrout, An-Nalah National University, Palestine.

The Third Circle to Makkah: From (*Min*)..To (*Ila*)..

The two other important words, in verse 1 of chapter Al-Isra of the Qur'an, **from** (*min*), and **to** (*ila*), summarise the twinning relationship between Makkah and Islamicjerusalem. Prophet Muhammad travelled by night **from** Al-Haram Mosque at Makkah **to** al-Aqsa Mosque at Islamicjerusalem. The author's argument may be summarised thus: *from* is the point of departure or the starting chapter, which is also the point of reference *to* the last point or the final chapter. According to Muslim belief, Makkah was the first chapter in the life of humanity when Adam built the first house of worship on earth. The final chapter or the relationship with earth will finish in Islamicjerusalem. According to the Qur'anic verses (e.g. Qur'an, 50: 41)[8] and the Prophetic traditions[9], Islamicjerusalem will be the land where the dead will be raised, gathered and assembled. From the Muslim point of view, Islamicjerusalem was the nearest gate to heaven as this is the route the Prophet Muhammad took to heaven.

In addition, we know very clearly that there is a close relationship between the Ka'bah in Makkah and al-Aqsa Mosque in Islamicjerusalem from the previous verse and from other Islamic traditions. The author would even like to argue that there is a twinning relationship between the two mosques. According to one of the authentic Hadith which was narrated by Abu Dhar, the close link between the two places goes back to the time of Adam, who was the first human on earth, to establish with his sons this physical and spiritual relationship. Adam was the first human to build al-Aqsa Mosque in Islamicjerusalem after 40 years of building Al-Haram Mosque in Makkah[10]. This was not an isolated instance; this link has been developed and strengthened throughout history. Prophet Abraham came to Islamicjerusalem and from there went to Makkah where with his son he raised the foundation of the Ka'bah. His immigration to Islamicjerusalem was a turning point in showing the relationship between Makkah and Islamicjerusalem. Prophet Muhammad reinforces and strengthens this link during his Night Journey from al-Haram Mosque to al-Aqsa Mosque. In other words, if Adam was the first Prophet to establish this relationship, Abraham and his sons rebuilt or renovated the two holy places in Makkah and Islamicjerusalem, and Muhammad was the last prophet to make that link very clear and obvious in his Night Journey.

This argument was supported recently by the young and promising scholar, Haithem al-Ratrout, in his article on 'al-Aqsa Mosque in the Qur'anic archaeology'. On the basis of his examination of the architectural planning of both the Ka'bah and al-Aqsa Mosque, he discovered that planning to be similar. In addition, his examination of the boundaries of al-Aqsa Mosque on the basis of its proportional resemblance to the Ka'bah, and the orientation in the plan of al-Aqsa towards the Ka'bah, led him to conclude that 'the plan of building one of them (Ka'bah) was a model for building the other (al-Aqsa Mosque).'[11] Indeed, this also provides more material evidence of the authenticity of the Prophet tradition which was narrated by Abu Dhar as discussed earlier.

Allow me to share with you one of the findings of this Circle Theory. The first global Muslim mission started with the revelation received by Muhammad in Makkah in 610 CE and ended with the collapse of the Muslim political system in 1924 in Istanbul. This was seven years after the British occupation of Islamicjerusalem. The distance between the Ka'bah in Makkah and al-Aqsa Mosque in Islamicjerusalem is 1292.5 kilometres, and the distance between Istanbul and Islamicjerusalem is 1269 kilometres.

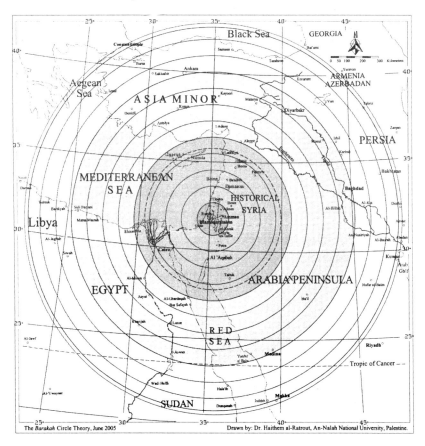

From the start, the Night Journey and Ascension experienced by the Prophet Muhammad established the centrality of Islamicjerusalem and its spiritual, religious, cultural and political importance. It assured Prophet Muhammad that reaching Islamicjerusalem would mean that the influence, impact and model of Islamicjerusalem would radiate, grow and expand to reach a global geographical location and people. It showed the international elements and effects of Islamicjerusalem and demonstrated that this could be not only an internal issue but a global one. Indeed, it established the uniqueness of this region and its effects on the rest of the world.

---

1   Abd al-Fattah El-Awaisi, 'the significance of Jerusalem in Islam: an Islamic reference', p. 50-51. Mohamad Roslan Mohamad Nor is developing the point about the land of the Prophets into a chapter in his PhD thesis, *The Significance of Islamicjerusalem in Islam: Qur'anic and Hadith Perspectives.*

2   This started out as a discussion with Haithem al-Ratrout during my several supervisory meetings with him for his PhD thesis research. We found that this might not be a relevant point for his PhD research. However, as part of developing the definition of Islamicjerusalem, the author felt that defining its boundaries would make a significant contribution to our understanding of the historical events of the first Muslim conquest. Accordingly, the author, as Othman Al-Tel's supervisor for his PhD thesis, suggested to him that he develop a chapter on 'the Topography and Geographical boundaries of Aelia (Islamicjerusalem) region', which became chapter two of his PhD thesis. Othman Ismael Al-Tel, *The first Islamic conquest of Aelia (Islamicjerusalem): A critical analytical study of the early Islamic historical narrations and sources,* pp. 41-68. Indeed, this helped him to resolve many of what had previously been viewed by many researchers and scholars as contradictions in Muslim accounts and sources regarding the first Muslim conquest of Aelia. This, then, was developed in August 2003 into a whole Master's dissertation by Khalid El-Awaisi, *Geographical boundaries of Islamicjerusalem.* From October 2003 to August 2006, Khalid developed this new finding into a PhD thesis, *The geographical extent*

of the land of Bayt al-Maqdis, the Holy Land and the Land of Barakah. His monograph (2007) *Mapping Islamicjerusalem: a Rediscovery of Geographical Boundaries* (Al-Maktoum Institute Academic Press) is indeed a major contribution to our knowledge in the new field of inquiry of Islamicjerusalem Studies.

3   Khalid El-Awaisi (2003) *Geographical Boundaries of Islamicjerusalem* (Unpublished Master's dissertation, Al-Maktoum Institute for Arabic and Islamic Studies), pp. 27-64; see also Khalid El-Awaisi (2007) *Mapping Islamicjerusalem: a Rediscovery of Geographical Boundaries* (Al-Maktoum Institute Academic Press).

4   "علیك بفلسطین و ایلیاء" M. al-Waqidi (n.d.), *Futuh al-Sham* (edited by H. al-Hajj, al-Maktaba al-Tawfiqiyah, Cairo), p. 31. Al-Tel argues that tthere are no reasons for rejecting or doubting' Al-Waqidi's account. Othman Ismael Al-Tel, *The first Islamic conquest of Aelia (Islamicjerusalem): A critical analytical study of the early Islamic historical narrations and sources,* p. 79.

5   Khalid   El-Awaisi   (2003)   Geographical   Boundaries   of Islamicjerusalem, p. 61; see also Khalid El-Awaisi (2007), *Mapping Islamicjerusalem: A Rediscovery of Geographical Boundaries,* p.274

6   The author would ask the reader to keep this point in mind about the Ottoman period since it is necessary to refer to it when discussing the Circle Theory later on in this chapter.

7   The main two Qur'anic territorial terminologies relating to Islamicjerusalem, *Al-Ard al-Mubaraka* and *Al-Ard al-Muqaddasa,* need to be compared with the other terminology, *Al-Ard al-Haram.*

8   Commentators say that the nearby place from which Israfil will blow his trumpet is the Rock in al-Aqsa Mosque. See Abd al-Fattah El-Awaisi, 'the significance of Jerusalem in Islam: an Islamic reference', p. 58.

9   See ibid., p. 57.

10   Imam Muslim *Sahih Muslim wa al-Jami' al-Sahih* (Beirut, 1978), 2nd edition, part one, p. 370.

11   Haithem al-Ratrout, 'Al-Masjid al-Aqsa fi al-Athar al-Qur'aniah' *Journal of Islamicjerusalem Studies,* vol. 6, no.1 (Summer 2005), pp. 1-36.

3

THE LAND OF (*AMAL*) HOPE DISCUSSION OF THE PROPHET MUHAMMAD'S PLAN FOR ISLAMICJERUSALEM

The history of Islamicjerusalem is a very rich and well-rooted one. This land has witnessed numerous nations, cultures and civilisations. Indeed, it could be argued that Islamicjerusalem is regarded as the most distinctive region on earth and quite different from any other place. However, rather than examining its history, this chapter will discuss this new terminology, the land of *Amal* (hope) and the steps taken by the Prophet and his first successor towards conquering that land. Particular attention will be paid to the Prophet Muhammad's strategic plan which he himself drew up for Islamicjerusalem.

Land of Hope
Before the first Muslim *Fatih* of Islamicjerusalem, Prophet Muhammad travelled by night from Makkah to Islamicjerusalem where he visited al-Aqsa Mosque. 'Glory to He Who did take His worshipper, Muhammad, for a journey by night from Al-Haram Mosque [at Makkah] to al-Aqsa Mosque [at Islamicjerusalem], which we have surrounded with *Barakah*' (Qur'an, 17:1). From the narrations related to this important event, one could argue that Muhammad travelled to Islamicjerusalem where he ascended to the highest heavens, returned to Islamicjerusalem, and from there went back to Makkah. Indeed, Islamicjerusalem in general and al-Aqsa Mosque in particular was the central point of his earthly journey, the Night Journey *Al-Isra'*, and the heavenly one, the

Ascension *Al-Mi'raj*. It was the place where his Night Journey ended and his Ascension began[1].

Muslims annually celebrate the anniversary of the Night Journey on 27 Rajab. A very interesting argument is still underway to determine the exact date of the Night Journey. A young scholar, Abdallah Ma'rouf Omar,[2] argues that it occurred in the middle period of Prophet Muhammad's Prophethood. The period between Prophet Muhammad receiving the first revaluation (Ramadan 13 BH/ August 610 CE, when he was forty years old) and his death (Rabi' al-Awal 11 AH/ June 632 CE, when he was sixty-three years old) was nearly twenty-three lunar years; half of this period is thus nearly eleven and a half lunar years. In short, it could be argued that the Night Journey occurred when Prophet Muhammad was in Makkah, eighteen months before the Hijra in the middle of the 11th year of his Prophethood/ 620 CE.

The author argues that the Night Journey and Ascension was a turning point for both Muslims and Islamicjerusalem and a very important starting point of transition in their history. It occurred at a harsh and critical time when the Prophet Muhammad and the oppressed Muslims were enduring all kinds of injury, challenges and persecution by their people and in their home town Makkah. This had become worse for the Prophet, especially after the death of his protector and guardian uncle Abu Talib in Rajab of the 10th year of the Muhammad prophethood/ 619 CE, and that of his beloved, caring and trusting wife Khadijah, his strongest moral and financial supporter who died two months after Abu Talib in Ramadan of the same year. The deaths of these two important and closest figures to the Prophet in one year, the year known as the year of grief, mourning and sorrow, added to his suffering and oppression. The Prophet had gone to Ta'if to seek the help of the Thaqif tribe; however, they incited their fools and slaves to insult and throw stones at him, injuring his feet so that they bled. In these difficult, hard and crucial moments, he turned to his Lord, complaining and seeking refuge, with the words,

O Lord, I complain to You of the feebleness of my strength, the scantiness of my resources and the ease with which people humiliate me. O most merciful of the merciful, You are the Lord of the oppressed, You are my Lord. To whom do You entrust me? To a distant one who glowers at me? or to an enemy to whom you have given power over me? If You are not angry with me, I do not care, but Your strength is more generous for me. I seek refuge in the light of Your countenance for which the darkness becomes radiant, and through which the affairs of this world and the next become good, that You may not be angry with me or Your wrath descend on me. You have the right to blame me until You are satisfied, and there is no Power or Might except in You[3].

After this very distressing event, Prophet Muhammad met with a unique prophetic experience in Islamicjerusalem. One can argue that the response to his serious, moving and emotional complaint came by his being transported on *Al-Buraq*, a supernatural animal, far away in terms of time and place to the land of hope. It has been reported that he was taken by night on a miracle journey from Makkah to Islamicjerusalem. As narrated by Imam Ahmad Ibn Hanbal in his *Musnad*, on the authority of Ibn Abbas, Prophet Muhammad met in Islamicjerusalem with the other Prophets where he led them in prayer in al-Aqsa Mosque. On the basis of this authentic narration, one can argue that Prophet Muhammad did not only travel to Islamicjerusalem in the Night Journey but arrangement was made for him to hold a unique summit meeting for Prophets in Islamicjerusalem. Several interpretations may be made of this narration[4], but one of them supports the author's central argument that Islamicjerusalem is not exclusive but inclusive, and should be opened up to everyone in the universe *Lil'alamin* as stated in the Qur'an, 21:69-71 as shown below.

As it was the land of hope for Prophet Muhammad, so it also was for Prophet Abraham. At the time of the Canaanites ruling over the region, Abraham was told to leave his home country and migrate to Islamicjerusalem; his own people had tortured him and tried to kill him, as stated in a verse in the Qur'an:

We said, O fire! Be thou cool and safe for Abraham! Then they planned against him, but We made them the greater losers. We rescued him and (his nephew) Lot (and directed them) to the land which We have given *Barakah* for everyone in the universe (*Lil'alamin*", *Al-Ard al-lati Barakna fiha*[5]. (Qur'an, 21:69-71)

According to this verse, the land of hope is not restricted to one particular group based on their religion, race or gender, but is open to everyone in the universe *Lil'alamin* without any discrimination. It is impossible to argue that Islamicjerusalem is the land of hope for Muslims only. On the contrary, it should be an open land to anyone seeking refuge and serenity.

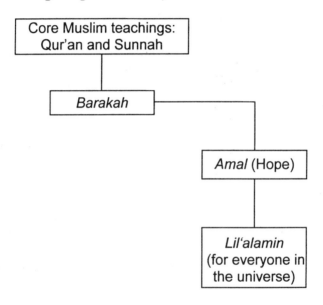

Diagram 1: Islamicjerusalem models for peaceful co-existence and mutual respect

On the basis of these two major events for Prophets Abraham and Muhammad, the author is introducing a new terminology or name for Islamicjerusalem, the land of hope[6]. Indeed, Islamicjerusalem was the location and source of hope and happiness for the early Muslims in Makkah where Prophet Muhammad encountered a new prophetic experience. Since Prophet Muhammad's Night

Journey, Islamicjerusalem has always been the location and source of Muslim hope. It has been closely linked to the Muslim faith, and has come to represent a living image in Muslim minds and hearts. It has also mobilised the souls, feelings and emotions of Muslims, attaching their hearts to it and making them yearn towards it. For example, the Muslims used to turn towards Islamicjerusalem when they prayed for a long period. This continued for another 16 to 17 months after the Hijra to Madinah, until the direction of prayers was changed to the Ka'bah. One can argue that during that period Prophet Muhammad used to turn for longer towards Islamicjerusalem than Makkah.

The Source and Beginning of the Change

The Night Journey and Ascension experienced by Prophet Muhammad established the centrality of Islamicjerusalem and its spiritual, religious, cultural and political importance. For example, Muslims consider the Prophet Muhammad's Night Journey as the turning point and the first step towards changing Islamicjerusalem, and consider it as a spiritual *Fatih* of that region[7]. This gave great hope not only to Prophet Muhammad but also to the oppressed Muslims in Makkah. In fact, it not only provided a temporary timely hope but granted a permanent hope, and a source and a step of change which extended their hope to cover expansion and growth of their geographical location. For the first time the practical international elements of their new message were shown to them, demonstrating that their message was not an internal issue but a global one. In addition, they were assured that, even if they were suffering for the time being, the message would not be restricted to the boundaries of Makkah or the Arabian Peninsula but would reach Islamicjerusalem. Reaching Islamicjerusalem, the centre of *Barakah*, meant, according to the *Barakah* Circle Theory of Islamicjerusalem (as discussed earlier in chapter two) that the message would radiate from Islamicjerusalem and grows and expands to reach global level. In other words, the new religion reached the transition stage to move from the local to global level through the centre of the *Barakah* in Islamicjerusalem. This means that hope requires making the effort to change to implement the vision and achieve its mission and aims. In short, Islamicjerusalem is not only the land of hope but also the source and the starting point for change to reach the rest of the world from the centre of the *Barakah*. It can be argued that if the change is a practical form of hope, so hope and change are among the manifestations of the *Barakah*, and accordingly, hope travels with the *Barakah*. It is, therefore, the centre for *Barakah*, hope and change.

The Start of the Change: Preliminary Practical Steps for Islamicjerusalem in the Prophet's Lifetime[8]

From this great boost to both Prophet Muhammad and the oppressed Muslims in Makkah, a new direction became apparent. Following this important turning point, a new agenda was born which led to the establishment of a strategic plan to conquer Islamicjerusalem. This meant that the Night Journey introduced new central elements for the future planning. The Prophet decided to establish this link and make its theoretical perspectives into reality. This was shown through the Prophet's desire to save Islamicjerusalem to the utmost extent. Indeed, Prophet Muhammad turned his attention to conquering Islamicjerusalem at this very early stage. However, he was occupied by other crucial matters to establish and spread his new message, such as the emigration to Madinah and establishing the first Islamic state there. This did not prevent him starting preparations for the campaign through the continuous raising of his companions' awareness to his strategic plans for Islamicjerusalem. This began by giving the good tidings that Islamicjerusalem would be conquered by Muslims. For example, Prophet Muhammad told Shaddad Ibn Aws, who died and was buried in al-Rahma cemetery in Islamicjerusalem in 58 AH/ 677-678 CE, that:

> Al-Sham (historical Syria) will be conquered, and Islamicjerusalem will be conquered where you and your offspring will be Imams there, if God wills.

Later on, during the Expedition *Ghazwah* of Tabuk in 9 AH/630CE, the Prophet Muhammad continued to send the same message to his companions. He also told Awf Ibn Malik (d. 73AH):

Count six things, Awf, between now and the Day of Judgement. The first is my death ... and the second will be the *Fatih* of Islamicjerusalem[9].

In addition, the city of Hebron was the first Islamic charitable endowment in Islamicjerusalem - indeed the first in Muslim history. Solid evidence attributes to Prophet Muhammad himself[10], namely, that he endowed part of Islamicjerusalem, in this case Hebron, to the companion Tamim Ibn Aws Al-Dari, his family and successors until the Day of Judgement. Companion Tamim was the first inhabitant of Islamicjerusalem to be converted to Islam, and he died and was buried in the north of Bayt Jibrin near Hebron in Islamicjerusalem. This making an endowment to him and his family after him until the end of this earthly life leads the author to argue that the Prophet was in fact making every effort available to him at that time to lay the foundations for his strategic plan for conquering Islamicjerusalem. Indeed, following the first Muslim *Fatih* of Islamic of Jerusalem, Caliphs in successive Muslim ages supported, recognised, and implemented this endowment. Muslim religious scholars, such as one of the most notably classic Imam Al-Ghazali[11], declared that any who 'oppose the correctness of this bequest and challenge it are unbelievers.'[12] Even the special court headed by Thomas Haycraft, the British Chief Justice, and Shaikh Khalil al-Khalidi, the President of the Shari'a Court of Appeal, in its decision 26/2 of 29 January 1927, ruled the endowment of the companion Tamim Al-Dari to be the one that "we regard as a correct endowment."[13] The British Mandate government in Palestine also recognised this endowment in a memorandum which the secretary-general of that government sent to the President of the Islamic Shari'a Council[14]. Indeed, the endowment was issued by Prophet Muhammad himself before the first Muslim *Fatih* of Islamicjerusalem. So, as argued earlier, this endowment is another clear indication of the Prophet Muhammad's plan to conquer that region.

However, following the establishment of the Madinah Islamic state, and in particular after the truce of Hudaybiyya between the

Muslims and Quraish, with whom they were at war, Prophet Muhammad in 6 AH/627CE sent several letters to the international leaders at that time[15]. These included his letter to the Byzantine Emperor, Heraclius. According to historical accounts, Heraclius had left Homs on his way to Aelia (Islamicjerusalem) to give thanks for his victory over the Persians, in which he recovered the Holy Cross. It is worth mentioning that the Persians initially defeated the Byzantines, then Heraclius fought back and defeated Chosroes in 625CE. The Qur'an records these events: it states that 'the Romans have been defeated in a land close by; but after their defeat they will themselves be victorious in a few years' time' (Qur'an, 30: 2-4). A modern Indian scholar, Abu al-Hassan Al-Nadawi, argued that 'these verses from Surat Al-Rom were revealed in 616 CE, and Heraclius's victory over the Persians was in 625 CE.'[16]

When Heraclius arrived in Aelia and said his prayers and vows, Prophet Muhammad's envoy Dahiya Ibn Khalifa al-Kalbi al-Khazraji came to him and handed him the Prophet's letter, which was read out and translated to him.

In the name of God, the most Merciful, the most Compassionate. From Muhammad, the worshipper and Messenger of God, to Heraclius, the greatest of the Byzantines. Peace be with him who follows guidance. I am inviting you to Islam. Adopt Islam and God will give you your reward twofold. If you turn back (from this invitation), al-Arisiyyin (your people who follow the Chalcedonian theology) will blame you[17].

Heraclius was not angry and replied politely to the letter. Several Muslim accounts relate that, when Heraclius wanted to leave Syria for Constantinople, he assembled his people and proposed following Muhammad and converting to Islam. When they refused, he proposed they pay him the *Jizya* tax. On their refusal, he proposed making peace with Muhammad and giving him southern and eastern Syria, while the Byzantines kept the remainder[18]. When they had rejected all his suggestions 'he set off until he approached al-Darb, when he turned toward northern

Syria, and said, farewell, land of (southern) Syria. Then he ran until he reached Constantinople.'[19]

However, some political and military positions in the region pushed forward the plan to conquer Islamicjerusalem to a new phase, through action to safeguard their northern front and the edge of historical Syria from the danger of the Byzantines, to destroy their eminence, and to show the Muslim strength. Fortunately, this occurred when the Muslims had already secured their southern front after Hudaybiyya's truce and the conversion of the ruler of Yemen to Islam. This led to several early attempts and tactics which occurred through major events in the Prophet Muhammad's lifetime[20], mainly: Dawmat al-Jandal between Madinah and al-Sham in 5 AH, and another in 6 AH, Hasmi, in the boundaries of al-Sham, in 6 or 7 AH/ July 629, Dhat Atlah in the Balqa region between al-Qura Valley and Madinah in 8 AH/ 8 September 629CE, the battle of Mu'tah[21] on 5 Jumada al-Awal 8 AH/ 629 CE, That al-Salasil in 8 AH/ 8 October 629CE, the Expedition *Ghazwah* of Tabuk[22] on 10 Rajab 9 AH/ October 630 CE, and the last Prophet Muhammad's mission, Usama Ibn Zaid on 26 Safar 11 AH/ 8 June 631 CE.

According to the new findings, (chapter two) the boundaries of Islamicjerusalem extended to reach Mu'tah. This means that one of the main early practical steps taken by Muhammad happened in Islamicjerusalem. Indeed, this battle should not be viewed as an isolated event in itself, but rather as part of Prophet Muhammad's plan for Islamicjerusalem. For example, one of the most relevant points of Mu'tah's battle in this discussion is a very important statement made by Prophet Muhammad when the Muslim army returned to Madinah. This occurred when the Muslims in Madinah received their defeated army with much anger and called out to them 'O who ran away' from the battle-field. At this moment, the Prophet contradicted and corrected the Muslim attitude, 'No! They have not run away, they will go to fight again.'[23]

In addition, the Expedition *Ghazwah* of Tabuk which occurred one year after the *Fatih* of Makkah was led by the Prophet himself. He stayed in Tabuk for nearly ten nights and returned in Ramadan, which means that he was away from Madinah for nearly two months. Although he did not engage in any battle with the Byzantine army, he used his stay in Tabuk to enter into *Sulh* peace agreements in several places on the way to Islamicjerusalem. These included the agreement with the ruler (chief) of the town of Ayla (Aqabah) , and the people of Jarba', Adhruh, Tayma' and Maqna. He also sent Alqamah Ibn Mujzz to one location and Khalid Ibn al-Walid to Dawmat al-Jandal. These agreements[24] were very important and crucial logistical steps to prepare the way later on for Abu Bakr's campaign to conquer Islamicjerusalem. It has been argued that, due to their strategic location, these agreements - especially with Ayla - secured the local supplies of the Muslim armies' need for food on their way later on to Islamicjerusalem. Khalil Athamina argues that these agreements were a very clear indication of the 'Prophet's (serious) intention to conquer the Byzantine land' which was 'a strategic definite plan which in no way could be to cancelled.'[25] To justify his argument, Athamina refers to the fact that 'the Muslim *Fatih* policy was a realistic matter which was produced by the high strategy of the Muhammad message.'[26] In short, this Expedition (*Ghazwah*), concluded the Prophet *Ghazawat*, was a very important battle on the way to securing Islamicjerusalem and could be argued as being equivalent to the *Fatih* of Makkah in its results.

Moreover, the thoughts and statements made after the death of the Prophet highlight and support this author's hypothesis that the Prophet drew up a strategic plan to conquer Islamicjerusalem. It has been reported that, when Prophet Muhammad passed away on 12 Rabi' al-Awal 11 AH/ 6 June 632 CE, some companions thought of burying him in Islamicjerusalem, this being the burial place of Prophets[27]. Although he is not sure about this account, this author is not surprised that some Muslims might suggest such a thing after what they had seen of the Prophet's plans for Islamicjerusalem.

In addition, the first Muslim Caliph, Abu Bakr, engaged in a process of consultation with his fellow Muslims to discuss how to continue the Prophet's strategic plan for the *Fatih* movement and draw up an action plan. According to al-Waqidi, to convince the Muslims Abu Bakr presented them with a very important statement from the Prophet. He told them that he would implement the Prophet's plan since he had died before he himself could accomplish it:

> You should know that the Messenger of Allah, peace be upon him, *'Awal* depend on (he made up his mind and decided) that he turned all his attention and efforts *Himatuhu* towards *al-Sham* but he passed away [before he accomplished it]… the Messenger of Allah informed me of this before his death[28].

It is also not surprising to learn that when the Prophet was dying, he continued to instruct the Muslims that Usama Ibn Zaid's mission (*ba'th*)[29] should go ahead and not be affected by his own serious illness or death. At some point in those crucial moments, he even told the Muslims in his Mosque 'O people, Usama Ibn Zaid's mission must go ahead.'[30] Indeed, this strong instruction did ensure that Usama Ibn Zaid's mission went ahead; he left Madinah and camped in the al-Jurf area. However, the death of the Prophet postponed the mission for a short period of time[31].

It has been reported that some companions engaged in serious discussions with Abu Bakr and advised him to cancel Usama Ibn Zaid's mission. To support their argument, they referred to two main elements, the situation in Arabia after the death of the Prophet, and the young age of Usama Ibn Zaid[32]. Abu Bakr was not convinced, and insisted that he would send him on the mission. It is reported that he told the companions very sharply:[33]

> I swear by Allah, I will send Usama's army as instructed by the Messenger of Allah, and I will not counter a determination (will) made by the Messenger of Allah, even if I will be the only one left in the town.

On the issue of the young age of Usama, Abu Bakr told Umar Ibn al-Khattab in an angry confrontation, after he stood up and held Umar's beard, 'May your mother Umar lose you! The Prophet commanded him and you ask me to discharge him.' Indeed, such a strong commitment by Abu Bakr demonstrates that he was well aware of the Prophet's plan for Islamicjerusalem. Indeed, twelve days after the death of the Prophet, Abu Bakr sent Usama Ibn Zaid's mission on 24 Rabi' al-Awal 11 AH. This was followed in 13 AH by another mission headed this time by Khalid Ibn Sa'id, before Abu Bakr arranged his main campaign which was to conquer al-Sham including Islamicjerusalem.

This development was a natural progress to these events. Through their combined effects, they helped the Muslims with their plan to conquer Islamicjerusalem. Although the Arabs before Islam knew the region quite well through their regular travel and contact with business and trade with its people, they began to learn more about the region for military purposes. They also began to familiarise themselves more in the ways they should adopt in their conquering movements outside the Arabian Peninsula and learnt how to secure their future needs from the towns and villages on their way to Islamicjerusalem. In addition, these events helped the Muslims to assess the Byzantine position and situation in the region in general, and their military power in particular. They also initiated the destruction of the prestige of the Byzantines, which was another step on the way to defeating them later on.

In sharp contrast, Moses' people who were persecuted in Egypt refused to follow his instruction to enter al-Ard al-Muqaddasah, Islamicjerusalem, which resulted in their wandering in Sinai for forty years. According to the Qur'an (5: 21-26), they were afraid to fight their enemy and told Prophet Moses to go with his Lord to fight instead. However, Prophet Moses, like Prophet Muhammad, died before fulfilling his mission to enter into Islamicjerusalem. Prophet Joshua, known in Arabic as Yusha Ibn Nun, like Abu Bakr and Umar Ibn al-Khattab, took the leadership and accomplished his mission.

In conclusion, one can argue that Abu Bakr, who at that time was the highest political and religious authority, on various occasions after the death of the Prophet showed his serious and clear position and his keenness to establish and convey his future direction towards Islamicjerusalem. This can be summarised in his understanding of the Prophet's vision for Islamicjerusalem. Abu Bakr was probably the only one aware of the Prophet's plan and intention. For Abu Bakr, as with the Prophet, the *Fatih* of Islamicjerusalem was a central strategic aim. Accordingly, it was not surprising that Abu Bakr should continue with the strategic plan which the Prophet had himself initiated, developed and implemented.

In short, the first Muslim *Fatih* of Islamicjerusalem, five years after the death of Prophet Muhammad (12 Rabi' al-Awal 11 AH/ 6 **June 632** CE), was a natural progression. These events helped to create a supportive environment which would help to establish and direct future events. Indeed, they were preliminary steps on the way to the great campaign which was launched and directed by the first Caliph, Abu Bakr, at *al-Sham* and crowned by the conquering of Islamicjerusalem by the second Caliph, Umar Ibn al-Khattab in Jumada I/II 16 AH/ **June/July 637** CE. It has been estimated, by both late and modern sources, that the numbers of those who entered Islamicjerusalem with Umar were about four thousand companions[34] and *Tabi'un*[35]. This estimate indicates that a good number of the companions felt that they would like to witness the concluding chapter of the Prophet's plan to conquer Islamicjerusalem. Indeed, if Prophet Muhammad's Night Journey was a turning point for both Muslims and Islamicjerusalem, the first Muslim *Fatih* of Islamicjerusalem was a radical turning point in history in general and Muslim Arab history in particular.

---

1   Abd al-Fattah El-Awaisi, 'The significance of Jerusalem in Islam: an Islamic reference', p. 53.

2   The author is very grateful to Abdallah Ma'rouf Omar, a postgraduate student, for bringing this argument to his attention. The author encouraged Abdallah to develop his argument into a PhD thesis on the plan of the Prophet for Islamicjerusalem.

3   Ibn Hisham *Al-Sira Al-Nabawiyya*, Part Two (Dar Al-Rayan lil-Turath, Cairo, 1987), p. 68.

4   The author feels this to be beyond the scope of this book.
5   Muhammad Asad translated the word *Lil'alamin* 'for all times to come'. In the footnote, he translated it as 'for all the world or for all people'. Muhammad Asad (2003), *The Message of the Qur'an*, p. 553. Others translated it 'for all people', see M.A.S. Abdel Haleem (2004), *The Qur'an: a new translation*, p. 206; Thomas Cleary (2004), The Qur'an: a new translation, p. 159. Muhammad Muhsin Khan and Muhammad Taqi-ud-Din Al-Hilali (1996), *Interpretation of the Meaning of the Noble Qur'an*, p. 402 translated it as 'mankind and Jinn'. Abdullah Yusuf Ali (2003), *The Meaning of the Holy Qur'an*, p. 327 translated it as 'for the nations'.
6   For more than a decade, the author used this new terminology to refer to Islamicjerusalem in his lectures. This inspired one of his postgraduate students to use and develop this terminology. Mohamad Roslan Mohamad Nor done so in his PhD thesis, *The Significance of Islamicjerusalem in Islam: Qur'anic and Hadith Perspectives*.
7   See the details of the Night Journey in: Ibn Hisham *Al-Sira Al-Nabawiyya*, pp. 47-53; Ibn Kathir *Al-Sira Al-Nabawiyya*, Part Two (Dar Ihya' Al-Turath Al'Arabi, Beirut), pp. 93-112.
8   On the basis of these findings, the author urged one of the taught Master's students in Islamicjerusalem Studies to examine and study the period of the Prophet and his plan for Islamicjerusalem. This is now developing into a PhD thesis.
9   Abd al-Fattah El-Awaisi, 'The significance of Jerusalem in Islam: an Islamic reference', p. 60. See also more of these indications on p. 54.
10   See Shaikh Muhammad Bakhit Al-Muti'i *Copy of the Ruling by His Eminence Shaikh Muhammad Bakhit Al-Muti'i, former Mufti of Egypt, on the Waqf of the Prophet's Companion Tamim Al-Dari and his successors*, issued on 7 Rajab 1350 AH, No. 275, p. 99, Part 7 (Islamic Vocational Orphanage, Jerusalem, 1984); Muhammad Ibshirly and Muhammad Dawud Al-Tamimi *Awqaf wa Amlak Al-Muslimin fi Filistin*, (Centre for Researches in Islamic History, Arts and Culture, Istanbul, 1982), which contains an investigation and presentation of one of the land registers in the Ottoman state in which all the Muslims waqfs and properties in the five provinces of Palestine: (Islamicjerusalem, Gaza, Safad, Nablus and 'Ajlun) were registered. These had been kept in Turkey since the tenth century AH (the sixteenth century AD), that is, since the Ottoman conquest of Palestine in 922 AH/ 1516 CE in the time of Sultam Selim I, in the

Ottoman Records House of the Turkish Prime Minister's office in Istanbul. See also Najm al-Din Muhammad Ibn Ahmad al-Ghayti *Al-Jawab al-Qawim an al-Su'al al-Mut'alliq bi Iqta' al-Sayyid Tamim* (edited by Hassan Abd al-Rahman al-Silwadi), (Islamic Research Centre, Jerusalem, 1986), pp. 44-45.

11   It has been claimed that Imam al-Ghazali visited Islamicjerusalem in 489AH/ 1095CE, a few years before the Crusader period. According to this popular public claim, he stayed there and wrote his famous book, *Ihya' Ulum al-Din.* It has been said that, during his time there, there were more than 630 Muslim theologians in Islamicjerusalem.

12   See Najm Al-Din Muhammad Ibn Ahmad Al-Ghayti *Al-Jawab al-Qawim 'an al-Su'al al-Mut'alliq bi Iqta' al-Sayyid Yamim*, pp. 44-45.

13   Shaikh Muhammad Bakhit Al Muti'i *Copy of the Ruling by His Eminence Shaikh Muhammad Bakhit Al-Muti'i*, pp. 9-10.

14   Muhammad Rafiq al-Tamimi *al-Iqta' wa awal 'Iqta' fi al-Islam*, p. 66, quoted by Abd al-Fattah El-Awaisi *Darih wa Masjid al-Sahabi al-Jalil Tamim Ibn Aws Al-Dari, Radiya Allahu 'anhu: 1917-1948* (Jerusalem, 1989), p. 20.

15   Such as his letter to Chosroes, al-Muqawqis, the Amir of Oman, Yamama, Bahrain and others.

16   Abu al-Hassan al-Nadawi *Al-Sira al-Nabawiyya* (Al-Maktaba al-Asriya, Sidon, 1981), p. 329.

17   Ibn Kathir *Al-Sira Al-Nabawiyya*, Part three, p. 501. In al-Tabari we have the following text for the same letter. 'In the name of God, the most Merciful, the most Compassionate. From Muhammad, the Messenger of God, to Heraclius, the greatest of the Byzantines. Peace be with him who follows guidance. Adopt Islam and be saved. Adopt Islam and God will give you your reward twofold. If you turn back (from this invitation), the ploughmen will blame you.' Al-Tabari, *Tarikh al-Rusul wa al-Muluk* (Beirut, 1988), 2nd edition, part two, p. 130.

18   Southern and eastern Syria consisted of Palestine, Jordan and Damascus, Homs and anywhere that side of al-Darb. On the other side of al-Darb was northern Syria.

19   Al-Tabari, *Tarikh al-Rusul wa al-Muluk*, p. 131. See also Ibn Kathir *Al-Sira Al-Nabawiyya*, Part three, pp. 505-506.

20   For more details of these events see Hani Abu al-Rub, *Tarikh Filastin fi Sadr al-Islam* (Jerusalem, 2002), pp. 93-94; Abd Allah al-Sharif 'Mawqif Yahud al-Sham min al-Fatih al-Islami', *Majalat*

Jami'at Umm al-qura li Ulum al-Shari'a wa al-Lugha al-Arabia wa Adabiha vol. 16, No. 28 (Shawwal 1424 AH), p. 502.

21 Mu'tah lies in the eastern part of the south of the Dead Sea, 12 kilometres south of Karak. The author had the privilege of visiting Mu'tah, the site of the battle, and al-Mazar where he stayed with his family overnight in the summer of 2004 for the first time. This visit gave him a better understanding of the sequence of battle.

22 Tabuk lies 700 kilometres from Madinah and south-east of Aqaba.

23 For more details about the battle of Mu'tah see Ibn Hisham *Al-Sira Al-Nabawiyya,* pp. 11-28; Al-Tabari, *Tarikh al-Rusul wa al-Muluk,* pp. 149-152.

24 Khalil Athamina, *Filastin fi Khamsat Qurun, min al-Fatih al-Islami hatta al-Ghazu al-Firanji: 634-1099* (The Institute for Palestine Studies, Beirut, 2000), pp. 95-96. The author feels that these agreements need a thorough analysis and examination.

25 Ibid., pp. 96, 98.

26 Ibid., p. 125.

27 Hani Abu al-Rub, *Tarikh Filastin fi sadr al-Islam.* He was quoting Ibn al-Ibriy (who died in 656 AH) in his book on *Tarikh Mukhtasar al-Duwal,* Catholic printer, Beirut, 1890), p. 262.

28 Muhammad Ibn Umar al-Waqidi, *Futuh al-Sham* (Al-Muhtassib Bookshop, Amman, n.d.), part one, p.5. This statement reads in Arabic:

"واعلموا ان رسول الله صلى الله عليه وسلم كان عول ان يصرف همته الى الشام فقبضه الله اليه ...

فرسول الله انبأني بذلك قبل موته"

29 Usama Ibn Zaid was the son of Zaid Ibn Haritha, one of the three commanders of the Mu'tah battle who died in that battle.

30 Ibn Hisham *Al-Sira Al-Nabawiyya,* Part four, p. 299. See also Al-Bukhari *Sahih al-Bukhari bi Hashiat al-Sanadi* (Dar al-Ma'rifiah, Beirut, n.d.), part three, p. 96.

31 For more information on this last mission of the Prophet, see Ibn Hisham *Al-Sira Al-Nabawiyya,* part four, pp. 253, 288, 299-301.

32 Usama Ibn Zaid Ibn Haritha was 18 or 20 when Prophet Muhammad died. He and his father, who died at the battle of Mu'tah, were very much loved by the Prophet. His mother was Umm Ayman, the nanny of the Prophet.

33 The author has quoted some of these discussions in his book in the Arabic language, *Makanit wa Tarikh Bayt al-Maqdis* (Islamic Research Academy, Scotland, 1997), pp. 34-36.

34   Although the author has doubts about the accuracy of this estimation; the figure of 4000 could indicate a large number of the companions rather than be an exact number. See the names of some of these companions in Arif al-Arif *Al-Mufassal fi Tarikh al-Quds*, (Al-Andalus library, Jerusalem, 1961), part one, pp. 95-100; Mujir al-Din al-Hanbali, *Al-Uns al-Jalil bi Tarikh al-Quds wa al-Khalil*, (Al-Muhtassib Bookshop, Amman, 1973), part one, pp. 260-267.

35   *Tabi'un* are the first generation after the companions, who did not see Prophet Muhammad but saw a companion of the Prophet.

4

UMAR'S ASSURANCE OF SAFETY (*AMAN*) TO THE PEOPLE OF AELIA (ISLAMICJERUSALEM): A CRITICAL ANALYTICAL STUDY OF THE HISTORICAL SOURCES[1]

The first Muslim *Fatih* of Islamicjerusalem in Jumada I/II 16 AH - June/July 637 CE[2] was an event both remarkable and long-lasting in its effects. It may be viewed as a fundamental landmark, not merely in the history of the region, nor even in Muslim history, but as an event which reshaped relations between the people of diverse faiths who inhabited the region. Moreover, its consequences contrasted significantly with the destruction, killing, and displacement that had characterised the region's history until then.

The arrival of Umar Ibn al-Khattab, who was at that time the highest political and religious authority and reference in the Muslim establishment, during the early summer of year 16 AH/ 637 CE in Aelia marked the beginning of a new and distinguished era in the relations between followers of Judaism, Christianity, and Islam. Indeed, the foundations for future relations between the three faiths were laid down during that historical visit in the form of what is known in history as *AI-Uhda al-Umariyya* or Umar's Assurance *Aman* of Safety to the people of Aelia.

A host of problems relate to the historical facts concerning the first Muslim *Fatih* and these have to be clarified and resolved. In the few academic studies on the first Muslim *Fatih* of

Islamicjerusalem, Umar's Assurance is regarded as being a major turning point in both historic and juristic terms. Nevertheless, historians, both past and present, have debated its authenticity and interpretation, while some of its versions have been used to support particular religious or political standpoints in the current struggle to gain control of Islamicjerusalem.

Far from being a study of the first Muslim *Fatih* of Islamicjerusalem, this is a critical, analytical study of the assurance *Aman* that Umar Ibn al-Khattab gave to the people of Aelia. It aims to examine and compare most of the available versions of Umar's Assurance, hoping to identify the version which could be argued to be the most authentic as Umar's original text. Indeed, these accounts differ in identifying Umar's Assurance of Safety in their texts, clauses, and the peoples they cover. Accordingly, this chapter focuses on the longest and most famous ones, namely the text given by al-Tabari and that published by the Orthodox Patriarchate in Jerusalem in 1953. In his efforts to ascertain the authenticity of these two main texts, the author has employed the historical methodology of examining historical sources. He has collected the most available related narrations, examining, comparing, analysing, and discussing them. In other words, he used systematic historical evaluation and synthesis evidence in order to establish authenticity and reliability. In addition, the author verifies these narrators according to their scholarly, religious, political, tribal thoughts and attitudes.

It is worth noting that the author does not intend to discuss what are known as *Al-Shurut al-Umariyya* or Umar's Conditions or Pacts by Ibn al-Qayyim al-Jawziyya, which are rejected by some researchers[3] and supported by others[4]. However, many historians have confused these two unrelated and separate documents, which have led to much confusion and contradiction in their discussing of Umar's Assurance[5]. Nevertheless, the author will attempt to find some explanation and interpretation of the questions and doubts that have arisen concerning certain versions of Umar's Assurance which contain restrictions, in particular the issue of the exclusion of certain people, i.e., the Jews from residing in Aelia.

Moreover, the chapter discusses the reasons behind the appearance of various versions of Umar's Assurance. The whole chapter responds to Daniel J. Sahas's claim that the first Muslim *Fatih* led to the 'emergence of an opportunity for the Christians of (Islamic) Jerusalem to contain the Jews, with the help of the Muslim Arabs, through the concessions granted to them in Umar's Assurance.'[6]

Treaty or Assurance

Before the author starts to examine this document, it is vitally importance to clarify its nature; is it a treaty or an assurance? Most modern Arab scholars and Orientalists, if not all discussed in this chapter through an examination of or a reference to their work on the first Muslim *Fatih* of Aelia, have described that which Umar granted to the people of Aelia as a 'treaty' or as an 'agreement'.[7] Although Umar or his commanders may have negotiated the surrender terms with the inhabitants, the final product was certainly not an agreement. The author does not believe that the terms 'treaty' and 'agreement' appearing in their work are accurately defined.

Umar Ibn al-Khattab did not sign a treaty between two parties, rather he gave the people of Aelia *Aman* an assurance of safety. If it were a treaty, as has been claimed, where is the name of the second party who signed the agreement with Umar? The simple answer is that it is absent in all the available versions of the document.

What the document contains in its opening and concluding paragraphs, especially from the early accounts which provided texts of the document, such as those of Al-Ya'qubi, Eutychius, and al-Tabari, highlights the fact that it is an assurance not a treaty. For example, al-Ya'qubi was the first to give the text; his first paragraph reads, 'This is *Kitab* the document written by Umar Ibn al-Khattab to the people of *Bayt al-Maqdis* Islamicjerusalem.'[8] A similar opening was given by Eutychius, 'This is *Kitab* a document from Umar Ibn al-Khattab to the people of Aelia.'[9] The al-Tabari version is not exceptional; his opening and concluding paragraphs read:

This is the assurance of safety *Aman* which the worshipper of God (the second Caliph) Umar (Ibn al-Khattab), the Commander of the Faithful, '*Ata* has granted (gave) to the people of Aelia.

The contents of this *Kitab* assurance of safety are under the covenant of God, are the responsibilities of His Prophet, of the Caliphs, and of the Faithful if (the people of Aelia) pay the tax according to their obligations. The persons who attest to it are: Khalid Ibn al-Walid, Amru Ibn al-Aas, Abd al-Rahman Ibn Awf, and Mu'awiyah Ibn Abi Sufyan.

In short, this document which Umar granted to the people of Aelia is indeed an assurance of safety *Aman* and not a treaty.

Early Accounts

The early accounts of Umar's Assurance, which were relatively close to the period of the first Muslim *Fatih* of Islamicjerusalem, are in general short, without a date, and do not include any restriction regarding the Jews. However, subsequent accounts that have come down to us contain actual detailed texts, some long and some short. Among the earliest historians to report the content of Umar's Assurance without any text are Muhammad Ibn Umar al-Waqidi[10], a native of Madinah who joined the Abbasid court, became a judge under the Caliph Ma'mun, and died in 207 AH/822 CE, and al-Baladhuri (died 279 AH/892 CE)[11], who reported it from Abu Hafs al-Dimashqi.

Among the early historians who gave abbreviated versions of Umar's Assurance, but without al-Tabari's restrictions, are al-Ya'qubi, the explorer, historian, and geographer, who died in 284 AH / 897 CE, and the Patriarch of Alexandria, Eutychius (Said Ibn al-Batriq), who died in 328 AH / 940 CE. Al-Ya'qubi was the first to give the text:[12]

In the name of God, the most Merciful, the most Compassionate. This is the document written by Umar Ibn al-Khattab to the people of *Bayt al-Maqdis* Islamicjerusalem. You are given safety of your persons, properties and churches which will not be inhabited (taken over) or destroyed unless you cause some public harm.

A similar text was given by Eutychius:[13]

> This is a document from Umar Ibn al-Khattab to the people of Aelia. They are given safety of persons, children (sons and daughters), and churches which will not be destroyed or inhabited (taken over).

Although both historians give abbreviated versions which focus on granting the people of Aelia safety and full religious rights, they differ in style and expression. The part about the people of Aelia in al-Ya'qubi' s version is in the second person, whereas the third person is used in Eutychius's version. In addition, it seems that neither text is complete as they do not refer to the *Jizya* tax, which is a crucial point in all the arrangements reached with the non-Muslims. Issam Sakhnini argues that 'the missing of this essential part' raises the question 'has al-Ya'qubi deleted other parts of the Assurance? or did these parts not reach him? so he mentions only what he knows to be the text.'[14]

The author argues that, if al-Tabari's restrictions were authentic, which we shall discuss below, particularly that concerning the exclusion of Jews from residing in Islamicjerusalem, Eutychius would have mentioned them. He was a Christian in doctrinal disagreement with Sophronius, the Patriarch of Aelia (he took this post in December 634CE and died in 17AH/ 638CE, a few months after the *Fatih*), who followed the Chalcedonian theology. Eutychius believed in the unity of Christ, whereas Sophronius believed in the Chalcedonian principle relating to the dual nature (God and man) of Christ[15].

Discussion of Time, Place, and Chains of Transmitters (*Isnads*) of the Assurance versions

As is well known in the historical methodology, according to their narrators and authors, historical sources reflect the general circumstances and socio-political developments prevailing at the time they were written. Indeed, the sources are coloured by the personality of their author, the time of recording, and local, political, and religious interests.

Early accounts, which relate the content of Umar's Assurance without any specific version of it, come from Hijaz, such as al-Waqidi's account, which is characterised by moderate Shi'ism, or Syrian accounts such as that of Abu Hafs al-Dimashqi in al-Baladhuri. Among the accounts which report the content of Umar's Assurance without giving any text, the author is inclined to accept that of Abu Hafs al-Dimashqi as quoted by al-Baladhuri, as this seems the most accurate short account. Compared with the accounts emanating from Hijaz and Kufa, the Syrian accounts of the Muslim *Futuhat* in Greater Syria are, generally speaking, outstanding narrations from the most reliable sources. Apart from containing rare and detailed information, they are closer to the places where the events occurred, so the authors had precise knowledge of the Muslim *Futuhat* and their secrets. Hussain Atwan argues that the Syrian accounts are unusually long and detailed and that 'they differ from the Hijazi and Iraqi accounts in some aspects of time and place'. Nevertheless, the Syrian accounts 'concur a little with the Hijazi and Iraqi accounts in their historical framework and internal content, but differ widely with them on other points.'[16] If the Syrian and Hijazi accounts of Umar's Assurance are brief and general, the Kufic accounts are longer and more detailed. Indeed, the accounts which provide versions, whether they be short or long, are mostly Kufic in origin, such as the narration of al-Ya'qubi, who had obvious Shi'ite tendencies, or that of Sayf Ibn Umar.

While the best-known Muslim historian, al-Tabari (died 310 AH / 922 CE)[17], provides a version quoted from Sayf Ibn Umar al-Asadi al-Tamimi al-Kufi (died 170 AH/786 CE), Ibn al-Jawzi (died 597 AH/1200 CE)[18], who seems to give the same account reported by Sayf Ibn Umar via al-Tabari, provides a text which appears to be summarised from al-Tabari's version, but without the latter's details and his major restriction relating to the exclusion of the Jews from living in Aelia. It may be noted in Ibn al-Jawzi's narration that he substituted Ali Ibn Abi Talib as a witness to Umar's Assurance for Amru Ibn al-Aas, who was mentioned in al-Tabari's version. This may be attributable to a mistake, intentional or unintentional, committed by the person who copied the manuscript we have of Ibn al-Jawzi's book[19]. Nevertheless, the historical accounts indicate that Ali Ibn Abi Talib was not present at the first Muslim *Fatih* of Islamicjerusalem, but was deputising for Umar Ibn al-Khattab in Madinah[20].

The fame of al-Tabari's version of Umar's Assurance as quoted from Sayf Ibn Umar al-Tamimi al-Kufi (d. 180 AH/ 796 CE) does not rule out the need to investigate its chain of transmitters. Fame in itself is no proof of authenticity, especially when acquired a long time after the event, in this case nearly 200 years. Thus it is not possible to rely entirely on its fame when tracing narrations. Before starting to discuss the narration of Sayf Ibn Umar, which al-Tabari quotes, it is important to know that al-Tabari was born at the end of 224 AH/839 CE and he began writing his history after 290 AH/902 CE and finished it in 303 AH/915 CE. Moreover, the first edition of al-Tabari's history was published between 1831 and 1853[21].

It may be safe to argue that al-Tabari was one of a handful of historians or possibly the only one who mentioned the version of Umar's Assurance together with its chain of transmitters. Some Arab researchers cast doubts on this chain of transmitters. Ali Ajin claims that al-Tabari gave 'a broken chain of transmitters which is without basis in the study of narration lines.'[22] However, the author argues that the Sayf Ibn Umar chain of transmitters is a strong and valid one. The narrations of al-Tabari came from Sayf Ibn Umar al-Tamimi al-Kufi (died 180AH), from Khalid Ibn Ma'dan (a Shami from Hims who was a *Tabi'i* from the first generation after the companions of the Prophet, died 103AH) and Ubada Ibn Nusai al-Sakouni al-Kindi (a Shami who was a *Tabi'i* and was the Judge of Tiberias, died 118 AH/736CE).[23] According to modern Arab-Palestinian historian, Khalil Athamina, Ubada Ibn Nusai was a Muslim jurist who was appointed as the governor of the *Imara* in Jordan during the Caliphate of Umar Ibn Abd al-Aziz, and was known as *Sayid,* the master of the people of Jordan.[24] A modern Hadith scholar, Musa al-Basit, who investigated the background of Ibn Ma'dan and Ibn Nusai, confirms that both these *Tabi'in* are safely considered by a large majority 'consensus' of classical Hadith scholars he examined, to be 'well known and trustworthy'. In short, one of these two trustworthy *Tabi'in* was a Muslim jurist and 'a trustworthy *Muhadith* Hadith scholar'[25] in his own right, who also worked for the Muslim political establishment at the time.

Discussion of al-Tabari's Version

In the name of God, the most Merciful, the most Compassionate. This is the assurance of safety *Aman* which the worshipper of God (the second Caliph) Umar (Ibn al-Khattab), the Commander of the Faithful, has granted to the people of Aelia.

He has granted them an assurance of safety *Aman* for their lives and possessions, their churches and crosses; the sick and the healthy (to every one without exception); and for the rest of its religious communities. Their churches will not be inhabited (taken over) nor destroyed (by Muslims). Neither they, nor the land on which they stand, nor their cross, nor their possessions will be encroached upon or partly seized. The people will not be compelled *Yukrahuna* in religion, nor anyone of them be maltreated *Yudarruna.* {No Jews should reside with them in Aelia}[26]

The people of Aelia must pay the *Jizya* tax like *Ahl al-Mada'in* the people of the (other) regions/cities. They must expel the Byzantines and the robbers. As for those (the first Byzantine group) who must leave (Aelia), their lives and possessions shall be safeguarded until they reach their place of safety, and as for those (the second Byzantine group) who (choose to) remain, they will be safe. They will have to pay the tax like the people of Aelia.

Those people of Aelia who would like to leave with the Byzantines, take their possessions, and abandon their churches and crosses will be safe until they reach their place of safety.

Whosoever was in Aelia from the people of the land (*Ahl al-Ard*) (e.g., refugees from the villages who sought refuge in Aelia) before the murder of *fulan* (name of a person) may remain in Aelia if they wish, but they must pay the tax like the people of Aelia. Those who wish may go with the Byzantines, and those who wish may return to their families. Nothing will be taken from them until their harvest has been reaped.

The contents of this assurance of safety are under the covenant of God, are the responsibilities of His Prophet, of the Caliphs, and of the Faithful if (the people of Aelia) pay the tax according to their obligations.

The persons who attest to it are: Khalid Ibn al-Walid, Amr Ibn al-Aas, Abd al-Rahman Ibn Awf, and Mu'awiyah Ibn Abi Sufyan.

This assurance of safety was written and prepared in the year 15 (AH).

The version given by al-Tabari, dated 15 AH, was until 1953 regarded as the longest and most explicit text, containing the greatest degree of detail of responsibilities, duties, and obligations.

I   Reshaping a New Society and Environment

To lay the foundation for the conflict resolution in Islamicjerusalem, the Assurance provides key arrangements to help in re-establishing and reshaping the new community in Aelia. It rejects the notion of supremacy of one people or race over others by beginning with an emphasis on the practical Muslim policy of the recognition of others by determining the inhabitants of Aelia's rights and the Muslim responsibilities towards them. It grants *Aman* safety for everyone who stays in Aelia, 'their lives and possessions', and for 'the sick and healthy', which means without any exception or discrimination, and for 'the rest of its religious communities'. This also includes securing their full religious liberty, firstly for 'their churches and crosses' and secondly for themselves as they 'will not be compelled in religion, nor anyone of them to be maltreated.' In addition, the assurance preserves and grants them protection for everything related to their holy places: 'their churches will not be inhabited (taken over) nor destroyed (by Muslims). Neither they, nor the land on which they stand, nor their cross, nor their possessions will be encroached upon or partly seized.'

In addition, rereading and interpreting this second paragraph of Umar's Assurance helped the author to develop the argument that the Muslim conquerors established a policy of non-interference in the internal religious matters of the people of Aelia. This means that the Assurance laid down the foundations for religious independence of each of the religious communities of Aelia. In addition, Othman al-Tel, using a linguistic approach, claims that this religious independence is offered to 'each Christian sect' in Aelia and 'is seen clearly' in the Assurance text; 'the plural form means the followers of the different churches.'[27] However, the Assurance was silent about employing non-Muslims in Muslim official governmental institutions. The Assurance did not mention 'any indication to prevent the *Dhimis* (non-Muslim)' from taking an official post in Muslim establishments in the region. Indeed, from the first Muslim *Fatih* of Aelia to the Crusades, there were many examples to prove that this was the case.[28]

II   Arrangements for Residing in or Leaving Aelia

As Al-Tabari's version lays down the responsibilities of the Muslim conquerors towards the inhabitants of Aelia, it also states the obligations of the inhabitants of Aelia. The first obligation was to pay the *Jizya* tax. The author argues that this tax was introduced in particular for the people of Islamicjerusalem to establish a two-way-traffic relationship. On one hand, to encourage the sense of belonging and the feeling that they were an integral part of the society through being involved in contributing financially to the welfare and development in their region, and on the other hand, as a means to commit them to the state. In return, the Assurance granted them the protection, safety and security of which they were in need. This important aspect is made clear in the Assurance from its opening and throughout. The word safety and its derivatives occur eight times, *Aman* (three times), safeguarded (three times), and place of safety (twice) in the text. Indeed, the *Aman* was the central theme for this important document. It emphasises the importance of this issue for the people of Islamicjerusalem at that time. The measurements mentioned in the text to secure this safety and security demonstrate how Umar was very concerned to resolve this crucial issue, not only for the local people but for others deciding to leave the land of Islamicjerusalem. Without *Aman,* one could argue that it would be difficult or even impossible to establish peace and stability in the region.

In general, the *Jizya* tax system was established in return for non-Muslim protection and security. In the language of our contemporary times, it is similar to some countries who receive payment from their citizens instead of military service. It is worth noting that not every non-Muslim had to pay *Jizya.* There were exemptions in the *Jizya* system[29]. In addition, Maher Abu-Munshar concludes his discussion of the Muslim jurist ruling on the rate of the *Jizya* by arguing that 'there was no fixed rate and there was room for flexibility depending on time, place, and economic situation.'[30] In short, the *Jizya* tax system was not a burden on the non-Muslim and was a great relief from the previous Byzantine tax system. In addition, the tax was less than the Muslims paid as *Zakat.*

While the first obligation of the inhabitants of Aelia was to pay the *Jizya* tax, the second laid down the arrangements to secure free movement for them. This second point was a necessary step to define and organise who should have the right to stay or leave after the completion of the first Muslim *Fatih.* A modern scholar, Issam Sakhnini, refers to al-Mushrif Ibn al-Murraja al-Maqdisi who estimated the number of Byzantines on the eve of the first Muslim *Fatih* to Aelia as being twelve thousand, and *Ahl al-Ard* as fifty thousand.[31]

The people who used to live in Aelia included its inhabitants and the foreign Byzantine occupiers, who did not belong to the same civilisation, culture and religious background as its inhabitants.[32] The text distinguished between two groups of Byzantines. In the first group were the members of the Byzantine armed forces, who were to fight on behalf of the Byzantine authority, and the robbers; and in the second group were the Byzantine visitors who possibly coincided their visit, maybe as worshippers or visiting relatives of friends, with the *Fatih* of Aelia. This classification is made clear in the text which, at the beginning of the sentence, talks about the first group and affirms that they should be expelled from Aelia; further on in the text, the second group is given the choice either to stay or to leave. Without this important classification, it could seem as if the text contained a sentence which at its end contradicts its beginning.

1. The first group of occupiers and robbers must be expelled by the inhabitants of Aelia. The common factor that prompted Umar Ibn al-Khattab to put the Byzantines and robbers in the same category is that they were all thieves and criminals. The Byzantines had occupied and stolen the land and its resources, and oppressed its people, while robbers had stolen the people's possessions. Indeed, both are major elements in causing problems, instability, and disturbing the public order and interests of the communities in Aelia. Indeed, one can argue that these elements were preventing peace, stability, and progress in the region. Accordingly, these people 'must' be 'expelled' from Aelia. The second group of Byzantine visitors were given the choice of leaving, or staying and paying the tax.

2. The inhabitants of Aelia, e.g., the civilians and their community and the religious leaders, are also given the freedom to either remain or leave with the Byzantines. For those wishing to leave with the Byzantines, the text allows them 'to take their possessions'. However, it lays down the condition that they should 'abandon their churches and crosses.'

3. *Ahl al-Ard* the people of the land (refugees from the villages outside the Aelia region) who sought refuge in Aelia at the time of *Fatih* are also given the freedom to either remain, or go with the Byzantines, or return to their families and houses. It is very clearly stated that they have been granted that 'nothing will be taken from them until their harvest has been reaped.' Indeed, this action taken by

the Muslim authority to take no tax from this group until they had collected in their harvest was a just one.

4. Finally, one could claim that it contains an expression that cannot be implemented: 'Whosoever was in Aelia from the people of the land (*Ahl al-Ard*) (e.g., refugees from the villages who sought refuge in Aelia) before the murder of *fulan* (name of a person) so-and-so.' Zakariyya al-Quda comments on this phrase: 'in a blanket form, without mentioning the name of *fulan* so-and-so or giving any clue to his identity or the date of his murder. Obviously it is impossible to determine to whom this description applies, so it is impossible to implement. It is impossible that this would be the text of a binding treaty.'[33]

The author argues that the expression 'before the murder of *fulan* so-and-so' may not refer to an unknown person, but to a very well-known person at the time of the Muslim *Fatih*. The author does not rule out the possibility that the name of the victim may have been transcribed incorrectly from al-Tabari's original manuscript. It could be *falak* or *falaj* or *falah* and not *fulan*. Therefore, the matter should be investigated using al-Tabari's original manuscript (which was not available to the author) before reaching any conclusion about the problem. Undoubtedly, the people of Aelia and the Muslim conquerors knew this person very well, which prompted Umar Ibn al-Khattab to mention his death as an important event that occurred during the *Fatih* and was familiar to the people at that time. It is well known that, in those days, the Arabs used famous events as landmarks in their calendar. Moreover, it would seem that this victim was neither an inhabitant of Aelia nor a Byzantine nor a robber, but a distinguished visitor to Aelia or someone who was a refugee during the Muslim *Fatih*. The clue to this is that his name appears after the expression 'Whosoever was in Aelia from the people of the land (*Ahl al-Ard*) before the murder of *fulan*.' This means that the murder frightened the local people (villagers) and drove many of them to seek refuge in Aelia. Although the author cannot make a categorical statement without examining al-Tabari's original manuscript, he refers to

Mujir al-Din al-'Ulaimi (died 928 AH/1521 CE) in his version of
Umar's Assurance; he does not mention al-Tabari's phrase 'before
the murder of *fulan* so-and-so.'[34]

Finally, a modern Arab-Palestinian historian, Khalil Athaminah,
presents a very strange reading of Umar's Assurance. He claims
that these arrangements, which he calls 'conditions' of the Umar's
Assurance, 'secured the evacuation of many buildings and houses
from its people; and left them empty so that the Arab Muslims
could take them over as their residences.' Furthermore, he claims
that 'these conditions alone secured the evacuation of a huge
number of Jerusalem's buildings and houses. This is due to the
large number of those people who should be expelled from the
city.'[35] Unfortunately, Athaminah does not provide us with any
historical evidence to support his claim that this was the case on
the ground at that time. Indeed, this is a curious interpretation of
the text of Umar's Assurance as it contradicts the main trend and
historical events of the first Muslim *Fatih* of Aelia. A young
promising scholar, Haitham al-Ratrout, argues that 'Indeed,
Umar's Assurance does not allow Muslims to take over Christian
houses in the city.'[36]

Abu Ubayed al-Qassim Ibn Sallam (died 224AH/836CE) narrated
in his book *Kitab Al-Amwal*[37] from Abdullah Ibn Salih (d.
223AH/838CE) from al-Layyth Ibn Sa'd (d. 165 AH/782CE)
from Yazid Ibn Abi Habib (an Egyptian who was the *Mufti* of
Egypt until his death in 128AH/746CE)[38] that it was agreed that
everything within the Walled City of Aelia should remain in the
hands of its inhabitants as long as they paid the *Jizya* tax. The areas
outside the Walled City would be in the hands of the conquering
Muslims. Al-Sakhnini argues that the Abu Ubayed narration is
unique and the only account in this regard which was first reported
by Abu Ubayed and then quoted by al-Baladhuri.[39] Indeed, this
historical event undoubtedly ties in with our forthcoming
discussion of Islam's attitude toward plurality, conflict, and justice.

In addition, Haitham al-Ratrout comes to a very innovative
conclusion using interdisciplinary and multidisciplinary approaches

in studying the historical sources on the subject, archaeological and architectural studies, and reports on excavations in Islamicjerusalem. Al-Ratrout argues that the area of al-Aqsa Mosque, on which the Muslims built the Mosque after the *Fatih*, fell outside the Walled City of Aelia.[40] Moreover, a respected modern English historian, Karen Armstrong, presents a leading argument on the Muslim attitudes towards Islamicjerusalem. She argues that 'Muslims made no attempt to build mosques in the Christian part of Jerusalem and showed no desire to create facts on the ground there until after the Crusades, which permanently damaged relations between the three religions of Abraham in Jerusalem. But until the Crusades, Jerusalem remained a predominantly Christian city and Muslims remained in the minority.'[41]

III   Exclusion of the Jews from Residing in Aelia

Although the previous examinations did much to convince the author that the al-Tabari version could be the most authentic account of Umar's Assurance of Safety, a restrictive added sentence prompted the author to have again, at the very least, doubts about its authenticity. Indeed, this is one of the most important issues which needs to be discussed critically, along with an analysis of al-Tabari's version and in particular its main added restriction, which together are at variance with the *Fatih* and its general trends. None of the versions preceding al-Tabari's mentions or supports this addition. This major restriction mentioned in al-Tabari's version is examined and discussed in this section.

Towards the end of the second paragraph of al-Tabari's version, we found a short sentence which contained only seven words in the original language of the document (Arabic) and eight words in the translated language (English): 'No Jew should reside with them in Aelia.' The structural position of this short sentence does not fit in with the contents of the whole paragraph which, as discussed earlier, focus solely on the practical Muslim policy of recognition of others through determining their rights and the Muslim responsibilities towards them. It talks about *Aman* for anyone who stays in Aelia, without any exception or discrimination, and secures their religious freedom and protection in everything related to their holy places. Indeed, this suggests that this controversial sentence was not part of the original document and was probably added for religious or political reasons.

Although it has been claimed that this restriction was placed on Umar Ibn al-Khattab by the inhabitants of Aelia, in particular the Patriarch Sophronius, it is not supported or even mentioned in any of the accounts preceding al-Tabari's[42]. Moreover, it would seem to conflict with the historical events and records known about the Muslim *Fatih* of Islamicjerusalem. The author has found no Arab historical source that confirms that Umar Ibn al-Khattab forbade the Jews to reside in Islamicjerusalem. If made during the rule of Umar Ibn al-Khattab, such a condition would have been implemented.

Karen Armstrong argues 'It was the practice of the *Rashidun,* when conquering a city, simply to endorse already existing arrangements and not to introduce major changes. It has been suggested that the supposed exclusion of the Jews may simply have been an initial step: the Byzantines had banned Jews from Aelia... Umar could simply have confirmed the status quo and, later, decided that it was not rational or just to exclude Jews from Islamicjerusalem.'[43] On the other hand, Daniel J. Sahas argues that perhaps the Islamic sources 'confused' Heraclius' expulsion of Jews from Aelia in 629 CE, when he conquered the Persians, with the version of Umar's Assurance[44]. However, there is another possibility, namely, that the Muslims had nothing to do with this exclusion and that it was an invention of Christian authors or probably added by a Christian source[45], such as Syriac chronicler Michael the Syrian, and the Christian chronicler Agapius (Mahbub) of Manbij[46], within the context of the traditional conflict between Jews and Christians. A Syriac source produced a short text claiming to be the assurance which Umar granted to the Patriarch Sophronius. This text includes a restriction that the Jews should not reside in 'Bayt al-Maqdis'[47]. A late source, al-Himyari in al-Rawad al-Mi'tar, states that 'the Christians made it a condition that Jews are not to be allowed to live with them.'[48] Greek sources indicate that the Christians wanted Aelia to remain a Christian area and this culminated in a clear sign to exclude Jews from there[49].

Jewish sources show that the Jews of Syria were 'patiently awaiting' the arrival of the Muslim armies because they were groaning under the rule of the tyrannical Byzantines and suffering their cruel oppression in the fifth, sixth, and early seventh centuries CE.[50] While the Jewish response to the first Muslim *Fatih* of Islamicjerusalem was 'characterised as generally positive'[51], because it terminated the Byzantine rule and liberated the Jews from their oppressor, some Jewish sources go even further. They not only state that the Jews welcomed and assisted the Muslim armies during the *Fatih* of Syria, but also claim that a group of Jews joined the Muslim armies, particularly during the siege of Islamicjerusalem[52]. Moshe Gil argues that "one cannot conclude from these sources that there were Jews in the ranks of the Muslim army.'[53] He also rejects the claim of Patricia Crone and Michael Cook[54] and makes the accusation that they 'exaggerate in seeing here proof of general Muslim-Jewish collaboration'.

Despite his doubts about the authenticity of the Muslim sources, Goitein describes the report of Umar Ibn al-Khattab as being accompanied by 'Jewish wise men... as quite feasible'. He justifies his claim by saying that it was their city before the Romans destroyed it, so it was 'atural' for Umar to seek the guidance of the Jews.[55] The author finds this twisted logic unsuitable for handling historical events. How could the Jews, who had been absent for five hundred years, guide Umar Ibn al-Khattab around a city which had been flattened and had its landmarks, elevations and undulations altered on more than one occasion? History confirms that the Jews, as well as other groups and peoples, entered Islamicjerusalem for a period of time and then left it. Their city disappeared conclusively, having been destroyed at least three times since the Prophet Solomon. Nebuchadnezzar destroyed the city, and the Temple, around 586 BC. The Romans destroyed the city twice and even effaced its name. The arrival of Pompey in 63 BC, according to John Wilkinson, was the 'beginning of a Roman effort to control the Jews, and ended two centuries later in the expulsion of the Jews from Jerusalem[56]. Titus destroyed the city and burnt the Temple around 70 CE, as did Hadrian in 135 CE. After the expulsion of the Jews from Aelia, Emperor Hadrian proceeded with his plan and issued his decision in 139 CE which stated that "no Jews should be allowed within the district of Aelia'[57], Jerusalem's new name[58]. From a religious point of view, Karen Armstrong argues that 'Jerusalem is not mentioned explicitly in the Torah, the first five most sacred books of the Hebrew Bible, and it is associated with none of the events of the Exodus from Egypt. Why should Mount Zion in Jerusalem be the holiest place in the Jewish world and not Mount Sinai, where God gave Moses the Law and bound himself to his chosen people?'[59]

A Jewish manuscript, preserved in Cairo Geniza and dating from the eleventh century CE, claims that Umar Ibn al-Khattab played the role of arbitrator or forceful mediator between the Christians and Jews in Islamicjerusalem. According to this document, Umar Ibn al-Khattab invited the Patriarch Sophronius and representatives of the Jews to a meeting he attended in person, so as to resolve the issue of Jews residing in Islamicjerusalem. After a long and contentious debate about the number of Jewish families who would be allowed to reside in Islamicjerusalem, ranging from seventy on Sophronius's side to two hundred on the Jewish side, Umar decided to allow seventy Jewish families from Tiberias to settle in the south of the walled city[60]. It would seem that this document was written during the reign of the Fatimid Caliph al-Hakim Bi-Amr Allah, who made life difficult for the Christians[61]. Apparently, the document seeks to remind the Muslims of the justice brought by the Muslim conquerors to Islamicjerusalem and the lifting of the oppression which the Jews had suffered prior to the first Muslim *Fatih* of Islamicjerusalem. Fred McGraw Donner quotes some accounts which say that Umar Ibn al-Khattab negotiated sympathetically about Jewish interests. Other accounts quoted by Donner say that Sophronius imposed a condition on Umar that Jews should not live with them in Aelia[62].

Furthermore, a letter written by Solomon Ibn Broham al-Qara'i, who lived in the first half of the tenth century CE in Islamicjerusalem, states that the Jews were allowed to enter and reside in Aelia from 'the beginning of Isma'il's dominion', meaning from the first Muslim *Fatih* of Islamicjerusalem[63]. Jewish sources also claim that the Jews were allowed to pray in Islamicjerusalem after the Muslim *Fatih*[64].

Christian sources claim that Jews resided in Islamicjerusalem immediately after the first Muslim *Fatih*. For example, Theophanes Confessor, who lived from the end of the eighth to the beginning of the ninth century, claims that the Jews indicated to Umar lbn al-Khattab that the crosses should be removed from the major churches on the Mount of Olives[65]. Moreover, the traveller Bishop Arculf, who visited Islamicjerusalem as a pilgrim in 670 CE during the Caliphate of Mu'awiya Ibn Abi Sufyan, recounts that he found two groups of Jews in Islamicjerusalem: the first had converted to Christianity and the second remained Jewish[66].

Michael Asif claims that small groups of Jews were already living in Islamicjerusalem and that these increased with time. By the end of the first century A.H., according to his claims, there was a large Jewish community in Islamicjerusalem divided into two groups, each with their own synagogues and schools[67]. In contrast, Shafiq Jasir argues that no Jews lived in Islamicjerusalem for the remainder of the rule of the four orthodox Caliphs. He quotes from a modem source, namely lbrahim al-Shiriqi in his book *Jerusalem and the Land of Canaan,* p.194, that the number of Jews during the Umayyad Caliphate (41AH-132/661-750CE) was about twenty males "who used to work as servants in the precincts of al-Aqsa Mosque."[68]

Karen Armstrong argues that 'It should also be noted that by the time of the Crusades al-Quds was known as a city of *Dhimmis,* because Jews and Christians were so populous and successful there. So certainly there was a strong Jewish presence in Aelia, even though most Jews preferred to live in Ramleh.'[69] In addition, the author argues that if it is true that Umar excluded the Jews

from living in Aelia, how could Salah al-Din and other Muslim
leaders have allowed them back? After the re-*Fatih* of
Islamicjerusalem by Salah al-Din in 1187, two new quarters were
created within the walls of the old city: the Maghrabi quarter and
the Jewish quarter with the Sharaf quarter in between[70]. According
to Donald P. Little, the small Jewish community in
Islamicjerusalem during the Mamluk period 'seems to have
enjoyed the status of *Dhimmis* granted to them in Islamic Law.'[71]
Joseph Drory argues that the Jews 'posed no threat to the Muslim
character of the town and lived peacefully with their neighbours'[72].
Donald P. Little argues that from al-Aqsa Mosque's documents
"We learn that the Jews were able to own property in the City and
to conduct business; on at least one occasion, moreover, the
Shaikh of Maghribi community intervened on their behalf against
governmental abuse.'[73]

Special Assurance of Safety to the Jews
A unique early Muslim account confirms that Umar Ibn al-Khattab
granted the Jews from Aelia a special assurance of safety. Hani
Abu al-Rub brings to us a very interesting reading of the early
Muslim sources when he states that 'Al-Ya'qubi pointed out
indirectly within his writings that there was an agreement with the
Jews. This has been confirmed by al-Waqidi.'[74] Indeed, this is a
unique account which Abu al-Rub quotes from Ala' al-Din Ali al-
Burhan Fawaz (died in 975AH). According to this account, al-
Waqidi stated that 'twenty Jewish individuals from *Bayt al-Maqdis*
headed by Joseph Ibn Nun visited Umar in *al-Jabiya* where they
requested an assurance of safety. He (Umar) granted them an
assurance of safety in return for paying the *Jizya* tax.' Abu al-Rub
argues that this assurance 'could be predicting to be a model for
how the Jewish minority was to be treated in the whole of
Palestine.'[75] This assurance of safety reads[76]:

In the name of God, the most Merciful, the most Compassionate.
You are granted safety for your lives, possessions, and churches
unless you cause public harm or protect who cause public harm.
Any one of you who cause public harm or protect who causes
public harm then he will not be under the covenant of God. I

distance myself from any action committed by the (Muslim) army during the military operation (13-16 AH/634-376 CE). The persons who attest to this are: Mu'ath Ibn Jabal, Abu Ubayda, and Ubai Ibn Ka'b.

Another Arab scholar, from a more classical theological school of thought in studying history, refers to an account related by al-Baladhuri (on the authority of Abi Hafs al-Dimashqi), who states that 'Abu Ubayda made *Sulh* peace with the Sammrits in Jordan and Palestine.'[77] This means that the Muslim conquerors granted the second assurance of safety to the Jews of Aelia but this time to the Sammrits living in the north of Aelia, in particular in Nablus.

Abd Allah al-Sharif argues that "The Muslim conquerors made *Sulh* (peace) with the Jews of *al-Sham* on the same basis as with the Christians except the Sammrits in Jordan and Palestine which have a special *Sulh* with them".[78] Moreover, he addes that al-Baladhuri related another account which stated that 'The Jews (in *al-Sham*) were to the Christians as *Dhimmi* paying *Kharaj* tax to them. The Jews, therefore, entered into the *Sulh* with them (Christians).'[79] In other words, what had applied to the Christians applied also to the Jews. This means that the Jews in *al-Sham* reached a *Sulh* with the Muslim conquerors through the *Sulh* with the Christians. Indeed, the Jews were insignificant in number; they were a very small minority during the first Muslim *Fatih*.

In short, as the region witnessed centuries of conflicts and exclusive attitudes to addressing competing political and religious claims, these crucial arrangements and changes were necessary and essential steps to provide a conflict resolution. They also affirmed the inclusive vision of Islamicjerusalem, namely to lead to the establishing of peace and stability in the region. Indeed, Umar's Assurance of Safety to the people of Aelia laid the foundation stone for the conflict resolution, re-shaping a new agenda for developing relationships between the followers of all the religious and cultural communities of the Aelia region.

Date of the Version

The date appearing at the end of Umar's Assurance, namely the year 'fifteen', has undoubtedly been added to the version and was not originally part of it. It is well known that the Muslims did not start using the Hijri calendar until the fourth year of the Caliphate of Umar Ibn al-Khattab, which was seventeen years after the Hijra. It is inconceivable, as Zakariyya al-Quda argues, 'that a document before this date should be dated with the Hijri date.'[80]

Discussion of the Orthodox Patriarchate's Version

One of the most significant versions of Umar's Assurance in which there are clear appendices and additions is the text registered under no. 552 in the Library of the Greek Orthodox Patriarchate in Jerusalem. On 1 January 1953 the Patriarchate published a new version of Umar's Assurance, claiming it to be a literal translation into Arabic of the original Greek text, which is kept in the Greek Orthodox Library in the Phanar quarter of Istanbul in Turkey[81]. The following is the English translation of the Orthodox Patriarchate's version of the Umar's Assurance as translated by Maher Abu-Munshar[82].

In the name of Allah, the most Merciful, the most Compassionate

Praise to Allah who gave us glory through Islam, and honoured us with *Iman*, and showed mercy on us with his Prophet Muhammad, peace be upon him, and guided us from darkness and brought us together after being many groups, and joined our hearts and made us victorious over the enemies, and established us in the land, and made us beloved brothers. Praise Allah O servant of Allah for his grace.

This document of Umar Ibn al-Khattab giving assurance to the respected, honoured and revered patriarch, namely Sophronious, patriarch of the Royal sect on the Mount of Olives, *Tur al-Zaitun*, in the honourable Jerusalem, *al-Quds al-Sharif*, which includes the general public, the priest monks, nuns wherever they are. They are protected. If a *Dhimmi* guard the rules of religion, then it is incumbent on us the believers and our successors, to protect the *Dhimmis* and help them achieve their needs as long as they go by our rules. This assurance *Aman* covers them, their churches, monasteries and all other holy places which are in their hands inner and outer: the Church of the Holy Sepulchre; Bethlehem, the place of the Prophet Issa (Jesus); the big church (Cathedral); the cave of three entrances, east, north and west; and the remaining different sects of Christians present there and they are: the *Karj*, the *Habshi* and those who come to visit from the Franks, the Copts, the east Syrians, the Armenians, the Nestorians, the Jacobites, and the Maronites, who fall under the leadership of the above mentioned patriarch. The patriarch will be their representative, because they were given from the dear, venerable, and noble Prophet who was sent by Allah, and they were honoured with the seal of his blessed hand. He ordered us to look after them and to protect them. Also we as Muslim (believers) show benevolence today towards those whose Prophet was good to them. They will be exempted from paying *Jizya* and any other tax. They will be protected whether they are on sea or land, or visiting the Church of the Holy Sepulchre or any other Christian worship places, and nothing will be taken from them. As for those who come to visit the Church of the Holy Sepulchre, the Christians will pay the patriarch Dirham and a third of silver. Every believing man or woman will protect them whether they be Sultan or ruler or governor ruling the country, whether he be rich or poor from the believing men and women.

This Assurance was given in the presence of a huge number of noble companions: Abd Allah, Othman Ibn Afan, Sa'id Ibn Zayed and Abd al-Rahman Ibn Awf and the remaining noble companions' brothers.

Therefore, what has been written in this Assurance must be relied upon and followed. Hope will stay with them, Salutation of Allah the righteous to our master Muhammad, peace be upon him, his family and his companions.

All praise to Allah Lord of the World. Allah is sufficient for us and the best guardian.

Written on the 20th of the month of Rabi al-Awal, the 15th year of the Prophet Hijra.

Whosoever reads this Assurance from the believers, and opposes it from now and till the Day of Judgment, he is breaking the covenant of Allah and deserving the disapproval of his noble messenger.

In order to ascertain the authenticity of this version, which is the longest and most recent, the author employed the same method of examining historical sources as that used by one of the leading Arab scholars in historical methodology, namely, Asad Rustum in his book *Historical Terminology* for ascertaining the authenticity of al-Duzdar's document. (Al-Duzdar is the commander of the Citadel.) When the problem of al-Buraq wall (the western wall of al-Aqsa Mosque) arose between the Muslims and the Jews, an international committee was set up to investigate this. A document surfaced that supported the cause of the Muslims. However, some opponents raised doubts about the authenticity of the document, so it was submitted to Asad Rustum for a technical, historical examination[83]. Using both external and internal criticisms that are well known in scrutinising historical sources, the author examined the Orthodox Patriarchate's document and found certain facts that prompted him to doubt its authenticity.

I   External Criticism

The author found the document to be written on relatively modern paper, dating perhaps back to the late Ottoman era. Although he was unable to examine its chemical composition, fibre distribution, and water stamp, the author found it to be written in different coloured inks, including black, red, and gold. Moreover, some lines are illustrated with various types of flowers. Such artistic decoration was unknown in the early centuries of Islam, especially in the first century after the Hijra, during the second decade in which the Muslim *Fatih* took place.

The document's foreword, body, and ending all contain vocabulary, expressions, and constructions not known at the time of the *Fatih*. Rather do these date from the era of Ottoman rule. For example, the author found that the document begins: 'To the honoured and revered Patriarch, namely Sophronius, Patriarch of the Royal sect on the Mount of Olives in Honourable Jerusalem.' In the body of the text it says: 'According to the obedience and submission shown by them (the *Dhimmis* or non-Muslims)' and, 'because they gave from the dear, venerable, and noble Prophet who was sent by God...' In conclusion it says: 'Whosoever reads *(kulluman qara'a)* this decree of ours', as though it intended to say: *'kullu man qara'a'.* These phrases do not conform to the style of writing prevalent at the time of Umar Ibn al-Khattab. As noted above, the document contains some terms that definitely date back to the Ottoman period. In the opening of the document the term *Ahd Nama* appears, *Nama* being a Turkish word of Persian origin meaning 'deed' or 'covenant'. In the body of the text we find 'O Lord, facilitate the affairs of Hussain', and at the end the term 'this decree of ours' is repeated. All these examples confirm that the document was written or invented during the Ottoman era - perhaps in the second half of the nineteenth century-or was at least translated from Greek to Arabic during the Ottoman period.

It is important to explain here that, regardless of whether this version was originally in Greek or translated into Arabic, it was undoubtedly written during the period of Ottoman rule, not during or immediately after the Muslim *Fatih* of Islamicjerusalem. Even if there proved to be a Greek text of Umar's Assurance, this would certainly not be the original version. This text was written in a very late period, namely the Ottoman period, in an obvious ecclesiastical style for religious and political reasons, as discussed later in this chapter. Moreover, the author has found no historical account indicating that Umar Ibn al-Khattab wrote any text or document in any language other than Arabic, nor has any historian made such a claim. Consequently, the author cannot depend on this document nor rely on it as being an original version because it is written in Greek.

Another reason for doubting the authenticity of this document is that the author finds its author does not adhere to the Arabic language and uses foreign expressions. The document is written in poor Arabic, using a style that was not familiar in the first century of the Hijra. The Arabs at that time wrote the word *Milia* with *taa marbuta* (ة ، ه) at the end, but in this document it appears with *taa maftuha* (ت). The same applies to the following words in the document: *al-Dhimmat, kafat, hadrat,* and *li-ta'at.* The use of *taa maftuha* instead of *taa marbuta* was common during the Ottoman rule of the Arab region. In addition, the document contains many grammatical mistakes. For example, '*al-Maghara dhi* (ذي) *al-Thalathat Abwab*' should be '*dhat* (ذات) *al-Thalathat Abwab*', and '*wa yu 'addi al-Nasraniyyu ila al-Batrak Dirham* (درهم)', should read '*Dirhaman* (درهما)'.

II   Internal Criticism

The author found that, at the time of the Muslim *Fatih*, Aelia was not known as *al-Quds al-Sharif* or 'Honourable Jerusalem' as it is referred to in the document. The name *al-Quds* was unknown at that time. Its name was Aelia, the term applied to it by Hadrian in 135CE. It would be logical for Umar Ibn al-Khattab to address the inhabitants using the region's name to which they were accustomed. Even if some traditions attributed to Prophet Muhammad are correct, the name used was *Bayt al-Maqdis* and not *al-Quds* or *al-Quds al-Sharif*, which are terms used in subsequent Muslim eras. In fact, the name Aelia continued to be used long after the Muslim *Fatih*, as demonstrated by the poetry of Farazdaq[84]. It is strange that the document exempts the Christians of Islamicjerusalem from paying the tax. The author has found no historical account or juristic formula that supports this exemption from the requirement applied by the Muslims after other *Futuhat*. The other unusual matter is that, at the end of the document, it is stated that the Assurance was given in the presence of a number of '*al-Ikhwa al-Sahaba*', or brother companions, including Uthman Ibn Affan. It is historically proven that the latter did not attend the *Fatih* of Islamicjerusalem and that he had indicated to Umar Ibn al-Khattab that he should not go in person to receive Aelia[85].

The author also found that the document states the names of some Christian sects, such as the Copts, the East Syrians, the Armenians, the Nestorians, the Jacobites, and the Maronites. It is known that at the time of the *Fatih* the only Christian sect in Aelia was the Greek Orthodox Church. At the time of Heraclius, which immediately preceded the Muslim *Fatih*, Aelia was part of the Byzantine state, where the teachings of the Eastern Church prevailed. Moreover, in the other versions of Umar's Assurance there is no mention of Christian sects in Islamicjerusalem. Early versions of Umar's Assurance focus on the general, without specifying one sect or another. This conforms to the method that prevailed at the time of the Muslim *Futuhat*. As for the mention of 'Franks' among the sects, this raises yet more doubts about the authenticity of the document, because the term was not known until the time of the Crusaders.

Not only does this late version mention the names of Christian sects that did not exist in Islamicjerusalem at the time of Umar Ibn al-Khattab, it also claims that these sects fell under the Greek Orthodox Patriarch. It states that they 'are subject to the aforementioned Patriarch and that he has authority over them.' Not content with putting the Patriarch Sophronius in charge of all other Christian sects and making them subservient to him, the document goes on to give him and successive leaders of his sect the right to collect one and a third *Dirhams* of silver from every Christian visitor to the Church of the Holy Sepulchre. This places the document in a new light. It would seem to have been invented some time after the Muslim *Fatih* to counter sectarian dissent against the spiritual leadership of the Church of the Holy Sepulchre. As for its attribution to Umar Ibn al-Khattab and its additions to the text of Umar's Assurance, these are designed to give the document extra weight in support of the Orthodox sect's leadership over other Christian sects.

The external and internal criticisms of this document have provided the author with several pieces of evidence that strengthen his doubts about the document's authenticity in technical and historical terms. He can conclude that the document is either forged or at least concocted during the Ottoman period. Moreover, his analysis of the document prompts the author to believe that the Greek Orthodox Church published it with these additions in 1953 as part of an inter-Christian struggle for control of the Christian holy places in Islamicjerusalem. Throughout the Ottoman period, especially in the 17th century and after, relations between Christian communities were marked by 'antagonism and dissension' over their respective rights in the holy places, which several times developed into 'bloody clashes'[86]. It was an attempt to give the Greek Orthodox Church priority and even leadership over the other Christian sects currently present in Islamicjerusalem. As part of this struggle, it has been argued that the Greek Patriarch Theophanius (1608-1644) was aided by his nephew Gregory, who spent three years in Istanbul 'forging assurance and pacts attributed to Umar' and other Muslim rulers[87].

After the end of the British Mandate rule in Islamicjerusalem and the end of the war in 1948, when Jordan took control of East Jerusalem, it could be argued that the Greek Orthodox Church in Jerusalem, which represented the majority of the Christians in the city, felt in 1953 that this was the right time to issue a new version of Umar's Assurance which would give them the upper hand over the other Christian communities in Jerusalem. As Jordan was the first Arab Muslim political regime after four centuries of non-Arab rule, the Orthodox Arabs expected the ruling Hashemite family of Jordan to show sympathy with their position in Jerusalem. Moreover, the last paragraph of the Orthodox Patriarchate's version warned Muslims against opposing it, 'Whosoever reads this assurance from the believers, and opposes it from now and till the Day of Judgment, he is breaking the covenant of Allah and deserving the disapproval of his noble messenger.'

Conclusion

The author does not agree with Philip Hitti[88] and Tritton[89] in their total denial of Umar's Assurance because of disparities between some accounts of the actual text. Nor does he agree with Shlomo D. Goitein, who considers that Umar's Assurance is a fabrication without any basis in reality because al-Baladhuri does not mention any text for it[90]. Indeed, it would seem to the author that Goitein is contradictory in his analysis of Umar's Assurance. He considers al-Baladhuri's account to be the most reliable, but does not accept the accounts of al-Ya'qubi and Eutychius (Ibn al-Batriq), both of which, he says, provide 'general, brief texts not significantly different from al-Baladhuri's account'[91]. The author agrees with Moshe Gil, who argues that "We cannot disregard him (Sayf Ibn Umar) altogether. The version itself (of Sayf Ibn Umar's account in al-Tabari) seems to be reliable."[92]

Undoubtedly the versions of Umar's Assurance have been expanded and embellished with the passing of time. The development would seem to have begun with al-Tabari's version, which he transmitted from Sayf Ibn Umar, and continued with the versions quoted by Ibn Asakir[93], through to that of Mujir al-Din al-'Ulaimi[94], and concluding with the Greek Orthodox version. This variation is probably related to Jewish-Christian relations, the development of Muslim-Christian relations, and Christian-Christian relations. A consideration of these versions within the framework of the developments of the social and political circumstances of the People of the Book from the time of Umar Ibn Abd al-Aziz to Haroun al-Rashid[95], the resolutions of al-Mutawakkil, and the historical events which followed, shows that the discrepancies, detailed additions, and conditions have, without the slightest doubt, nothing to do with the period of the Muslim *Fatih* of Islamicjerusalem, nor do they address the situation at that time. Rather they are part of the general conditions and the socio-political web that emerged there, which affected the position of the People of the Book and their treatment within the Abbasid state, to which we have referred above. New juristic ideas and formulae were drafted in response to the new developments that occurred in Muslim periods following the first Muslim *Fatih* of Islamicjerusalem. Abdul Aziz Duri argues that they dealt with matters that surfaced later. This led him to conclude that the text of Umar's assurance 'was developed to include conditions which have no relevance to the period of the *Fatih*, and that it received juridical formulation capable of meeting new developments.'[96]

In conclusion, the author is inclined to believe that there is no doubt that an assurance of safety existed and that Umar Ibn al-Khattab granted the people of Aelia an assurance of safety *Aman* for themselves, their possessions, their churches, and their religion, in return for their paying *Jizya* tax. This was in line with the general trend of the Muslim attitude to other areas in Syria or concluded with the People of the Book during the period of the Muslim *Futuhat*. As for additions and restrictions attributed to Umar Ibn al-Khattab, these are the products of later historical periods, resulting from socio-political circumstances that differed greatly from the time of the first Muslim *Fatih* of Islamicjerusalem.

Of the two longest and most famous versions of Umar's Assurance, the one published by the Orthodox Patriarchate in Jerusalem in 1953 demonstrates discrepancies, additions and restrictions. It is possible to argue with some confidence that this particular document is either forged or at least concocted. However, despite the author's major reservation towards one added restrictive sentence related to the Jews, he is satisfied that Sayf Ibn Umar's account which was reported by al-Tabari but without this added restrictive sentence, is Umar's original text that he wrote and witnessed.

In addition, this chapter totally rejects the claim made by Daniel J. Sahas that the first Muslim *Fatih* led to the 'emergence of an opportunity for the Christians of Islamicjerusalem to contain the Jews, with the help of the Muslim Arabs, through the concessions granted to them in Umar's Assurance'[97]. The question that arises here is: what grounds would the Christians of Islamicjerusalem have for containing the Jews, when they themselves had forbidden them residence in Aelia for several centuries and expelled them from it? If this assertion were true, why did the Patriarch Sophronius ask Umar Ibn al-Khattab to renew Hadrian's law and forbid the Jews residence in Aelia? His request was rejected by Umar Ibn al-Khattab. The concessions that the conquering Muslims granted the inhabitants of Aelia were not requested by the Christians of Islamicjerusalem, but were a gift from the Caliph of the Muslims to the people of that region, based on the principles laid down by Islam for dealing with non-Muslims, particularly the People of the Book. Sahas made his claim based on a text translated from the Greek which closely resembles the Orthodox Patriarchate's text of Umar's Assurance. The author has proved that this was fabricated or concocted to serve the political and religious aims of the Greek Orthodox sect in Jerusalem.

Although there were very few Jews living in Aelia at the time of the *Fatih*, they were also granted the same concessions as the

Christians which, summarised, gave them safety for themselves, their possessions, synagogues, and religion in exchange for paying the *Jizya* tax. Indeed, this important action to bring the Jews back helped to develop the reshaping of a new society in Aelia. The concluding operations of the first Muslim *Fatih* of Aelia put an end to the traditional conflict between Christians and the Jews. The Muslim conquerors' new agenda and frame of reference for Islamicjerusalem enabled the followers of the three religions branching from Abraham to flourish and to live and interact with one another for the first time in peace and harmony. Indeed, it led to the emergence of the Islamicjerusalem multicultural society. This was a major turning point for the region and the people living there and proves that inclusiveness and diversity in Aelia communities and society were a strength and not a threat.

Even if other religions regarded the acquisition of Jerusalem as 'an aim which threatened other People of the Book and competed with them'[98], Islamicjerusalem was not an exclusive region under Muslim rule. The arrival of Umar in Islamicjerusalem marked the start of a golden age and the beginning of a new era in which the region became an open one for all the nations. Karen Armstrong argues that Umar was 'faithful to the Islamic inclusive vision. Unlike the Jews and Christians, Muslims did not attempt to exclude others from Jerusalem's holiness' and, instead of excluding these religions in Islamicjerusalem, 'Muslims were being taught to venerate them'. In addition, Armstrong argues that 'from the first, Muslims showed that the veneration of sacred space did not have to mean conflict, enmity, killing ... and exclusion of others ... From the start, the Muslims developed an inclusive vision of Jerusalem which did not deny the presence and devotion of others, but respected their rights and celebrated plurality and co-existence. This inclusive vision of holiness is sorely needed by the people of Jerusalem today.'[99]

In short, the attitude of *Fatih*, or what I shall term at the end of this article **'the first Muslim liberation of Islamicjerusalem'**, was contrary to that of both Jews and Christians towards Aelia. The Muslims liberated the Christians from the Byzantine occupiers of Aelia, rid the Jews of the Byzantine oppression, restored their presence in that region after an absence of five hundred years[100], enabled all the communities to live side by side peacefully for the first time after a long history of conflict, and provided the grounds to establish Islamicjerusalem as a model for multiculturalism. These events in general, and Umar's Assurance, coincided with the core Muslim teachings based on the constructive argumentation methodology, the methodology of *Tadafu'* (counteraction), and the concept of *'Adl* (justice) based not only on the plurality and recognition of others, but on determining their rights, duties, treatment, and means of co-existence.

This final chapter in the first Muslim *Fatih* is attributed to the Prophet's companions, especially the second Muslim Caliph, Umar Ibn al-Khattab, who at that time was the highest political and religious authority and reference in the Muslim establishment. Indeed, Umar's Assurance of Safety was the jewel of the first Muslim *Fatih* of Aelia, and the beacon for developing Islamicjerusalem's unique and creative vision and nature. It not only rejected the notion of the supremacy of one people or race over others, but presented Islamicjerusalem as a model for multiculturalism and also as a model for conflict resolution.

---

1   This chapter originally appeared as an article in the *Journal of Islamicjerusalem Studies* vol. 3, no. 2 (Summer 2000), pp. 47-89. However, the current chapter has been substantially reviewed and revised which has led to new findings. In the light of new evidence and the latest research produced or published since 2000 in the field of Islamicjerusalem Studies, the author has developed and even changed a number of his previous thoughts and arguments on the subject and distanced himself from them. In short, as in the case of Imam al-Shafi'i, his article of 2000 should be known as his 'old argument', and this chapter should be known as his 'new argument'.

2   Othman Ismael Al-Tel (2003), *The first Islamic conquest of Aelia (Islamicjerusalem): A critical analytical study of the early Islamic historical narrations and sources,* p. 118. Jumada First or Second 16 AH is June

or July 637 CE (e.g., 29 Jumada First 16 AH/ 1 July 637 CE) and not March or April as stated by Al-Tel.

3   Maher Younes Abu-Munshar (2003), *A Historical Study of Muslim Treatment of Christians in Islamicjerusalem at the Time of Umar Ibn al-Khattab and Salah al-Din with Special Reference to the Islamic Value of Justice*, (unpublished PhD thesis, Al-Maktoum Institute for Arabic and Islamic Studies), pp. 97-121; Zakariyya al-Quda (1987), 'Mu'ahadit Fatih Bayt al-Maqdis: al-Uhda al-Umariyya' in Muhammad Adnan al-Bakhit and Ihsan Abass (eds), *Bilad al-Sham fi Sadir al-Islam*, (University of Jordan and University of Yarmuk, Jordan), vol. 2, pp. 279-283. See also Issam Sakhnini (2001), *Ahd Ilya wa al-Shurut al-Umariyya* (Amman), pp. 87-163.

4   Ali Ajin (1417 AH), 'Al-Uhda al-Umariyya', *Al-Hikma Journal* (no. 10), pp. 75-87.

5   See for example Khalil Athamina (2000), *Filastin fi Khamsat Qurun, min al-Fatth al-Islami hatta al-Ghazu al-Firaniji: 634-1099*, pp. 392-393.

6   Daniel J. Sahas (1994), 'Patriarch Sophronious, Umar Ibn al-Khattab and the Conquest of Jerusalem', in Hadia Dajani-Shakeel and Burhan Dajani, *Al-Sira' al-Islami al-Faranji ala Filastin fi al-Qurun al-Wasta (The Islamic - Frankish (Ifranj) conflict over Palestine during the Middle Ages* (The Institute for Palestine Studies, Beirut), p. 54.

7   See for example, Zakariyya al-Quda 'Mu'ahadit Fatih Bayt al-Maqdis: al-Uhda al-Umariyya', p. 276.; Hani Abu al-Rub (2002), *Tarikh Filastin fi sadr al-Islam*, p. 137; Khalil Athamina, *Filastin fi Khamsat Qurun, min al-Fatth al-Islami hatta al-Ghazu al-Firaniji: 634-1099*, p. 70; Moshe Gil (1992), *A History of Palestine: 634-1099* (Cambridge University Press), p. 73.

8   Al-Ya'qubi (1960), *Tarikh al-Ya'qubi* (Beirut), part two, pp. 46, 167.

9   Said Ibn al-Batriq (Eutychius) (1905), *Al-Tarikh al-Majmu'* (Beirut), part two, p. 16.

10   Muhammad Ibn Umar al-Waqidi (1954), *Futuh al-Sham* (Cairo), part one, pp. 214, 242.

11   Muhammad al-Baladhuri (1936), *Futuh al-Buldan* (Cairo), part one, pp. 114-145.

12   Al-Ya'qubi, *Tarikh al-Ya'qubi*, part two, pp. 46, 167.

13   Said Ibn al-Batriq (Eutychius), *Al-Tarikh al-Majmu'* , part two, p. 16.

14   Issam Sakhnini, *Ahd Ilya wa al-Shurut al-Umariyya*, p. 68.

15   Daniel J. Sahas 'Patriarch Sophronious, Umar Ibn al-Khattab and the Conquest of Jerusalem', p. 65.

16 Hussain Atwan (1986), *al-Riwaiyat al-Tarikhia fi Bilad al-Sham fi al-Asr al-Amawi* (Amman), pp. 231-232.

17 Al-Tabari (1960), *Tarikh al-Rusul wa al-Muluk* (Cairo), part one, pp. 2399, 2405-2406.

18 Ibn al-Jawzi (1979), *Fada 'il al-Quds* (Beirut), pp. 123-124.

19 Some investigation needs to be made concerning this person's identity and whether he had any links with Shi'ite Islam before concluding that it was an intentional mistake.

20 Al-Waqidi, *Futuh al-Sham*, p. 236.

21 Abd al-Rahman al-Azawi (1989), *Al-Tabari* (Baghdad), p. 134.

22 Ali Ajin 'Al-Uhda al-Umariyya', p. 71.

23 Musa Isma'il al-Basit (2001), *al-Uhda al-Umariyya bayn al-Qubul wa al-Rad: Dirasah Naqdiyyah* (Jerusalem), pp. 37-38, 99-100.

24 Khalil Athamina, *Filastin fi Khamsat Qurun, min al-Fatth al-Islami hatta al-Ghazu al-Firaniji: 634-1099*, p. 55.

25 Issam Sakhnini, *Ahd Ilya wa al-Shurut al-Umariyya*, p. 62.

26 This issue will be discuses later on in this chapter.

27 Othman Ismael Al-Tel, *The first Islamic conquest of Aelia (Islamicjerusalem): A critical analytical study of the early Islamic historical narrations and sources*, p. 229.

28 Khalil Athamina, *Filastin fi Khamsat Qurun, min al-Fatth al-Islami hatta al-Ghazu al-Firaniji: 634-1099*, pp. 138-142.

29 Maher Abu-Munshar presented a discussion on the *Jizya*. See Maher Abu-Munshar, *A historical study of Muslim treatment of Christians in Islamicjerusalem at the time of Umar Ibn al-Khattab and Salah al-Din with special reference to the Islamic value of justice*, pp. 57-69.

30 Ibid., p. 62.

31 Issam Sakhnini, *Ahd Ilya wa al-Shurut al-Umariyya*, p. 51.

32 Khalil Athamina, *Filastin fi Khamsat Qurun, min al-Fatth al-Islami hatta al-Ghazu al-Firaniji: 634-1099*, pp. 119-120.

33 Zakariyya al-Quda 'Mu'ahadit Fatih Bayt al-Maqdis: al-Uhda al-Umariyya', p. 276.

34 Mujir al-Din al-'Ulaimi (1977), *AI-Uns al-Jalil bi tarikh al-Quds wa al-Khalil* (Amman), part one, pp. 253-254.

35 Khalil Athamina, *Filastin fi Khamsat Qurun, min al-Fatth al-Islami hatta al-Ghazu al-Firaniji: 634-1099*, pp. 70-71.

36 Haitham al-Ratrout (2004), *The architectural development of al-Aqsa Mosque in the early Islamic period: Sacred architecture in the shape of the 'Holy'* (Al-Maktoum Institute Academic Press), p. 215.

37 Abu Ubayed al-Qasim Ibn Sallam (1986), *Kitab Al-Amwal* (Beirut), p. 168.
38 Sakhnini, *Ahd Ilya wa al-Shurut al-Umariyya*, p. 40.
39 Ibid., pp. 43-44.
40 Haitham al-Ratrout, *The architectural development of al-Aqsa Mosque in the early Islamic period: Sacred architecture in the shape of the 'Holy'*, pp. 209-239. One of his hypotheses in his doctoral thesis was to ascertain whether the area of Al-Aqsa Mosque, on which the Muslims built the Mosque after the conquest, fell outside or within the Walled City of Aelia.
41 Karen Armstrong (1997), 'Sacred Space: the Holiness of Islamicjerusalem', *Journal of Islamicjerusalem Studies* (vol. I, no. I, Winter 1997), pp. 14-15.
42 This new finding about the issue of excluding the Jews from residing in Islamicjerusalem is in considerable contrast to the author's previous argument. He argued that 'Umar Ibn al-Khattab did not oppose a provision in his Assurance – as requested by the inhabitants of Aelia – that "none of the Jews should live in Aelia with them". This guarantee was in conformity with the Jews' position in Jerusalem, which had been decided since Emperor Hadrian issued his decree in 139 AD forbidding the Jews to enter Jerusalem, living there, coming near it or even looking at it from afar. Umar renewed the decree of Hadrian, but allowed them concessions, that they could look on, and visit the city. This they did …. Umar's ruling ensured that, during the period when it applied, Jews had no sovereignty over Jerusalem. It certainly seems that it was not long after the beginning of Muslim rule that Jews did settle in Jerusalem again after 500 years of prohibition.' In the light of new evidence and the latest research produced or published since 1998 in the field of Islamicjerusalem Studies, the author has changed his previous argument on this point and distanced himself from it. See this previous argument in Abd al-Fattah El-Awaisi (1998), 'The significance of Jerusalem in Islam: an Islamic reference', p. 62.
43 Karen Armstrong's communication with the *Journal of Islamicjerusalem Studies.*
44 Daniel J. Sahas 'Patriarch Sophronious, Umar Ibn al-Khattab and the Conquest of Jerusalem', pp. 70-71. For the stance taken by Heraclius towards the Jews in Aelia, see Karen Armstrong (1996), *A*

History of Jerusalem: One City. Three Faiths, (HarperCollins Publishers, London), pp. 215, 233.

[45] Abdul Aziz Duri (1989), 'Jerusalem in the Early Islamic period: 7th - 11th centuries AD' in K.J. Asali (ed.), *Jerusalem in History* (Scorpion Publishing, Essex), p. 107.

[46] Ibid, p. 107; see also Moshe Gil, *A History of Palestine: 634- 1099,* p. 56. Gil argues that as "one might anticipate, the subject of Jews appeared important to almost all the Christian chroniclers.'

[47] Jean Baptiste Chabot (editor), *Chronique de Michael le Syrein* (Paris: 1899-1919), (Bruxelles: 1963), vol. 2, p. 425 quoted by Hani Abu al-Rub, *Tarikh Filastin fi sadr al-Islam,* p. 138.

[48] Abdul Aziz Duri 'Jerusalem in the Early Islamic period: 7th-11th centuries AD', p. 107.

[49] Daniel J. Sahas 'Patriarch Sophronious, Umar fun al-Khattab and the Conquest of Jerusalem', p. 67. Moshe Gil, *A History of Palestine: 634-1099,* p. 70.

[50] Israel Ben Zeev (Abu Zuaib) (1976), *Ka'ab al-Ahbar: Jews and Judaism in the Islamic Tradition* (Jerusalem), p. 35.

[51] Abd Allah al-Sharif (1424 AH), 'Mawqif Yahud al-Sham min al-Fatih al-Islami', *Majalat Jami'at Umm al-qura li Ulum al-Shari'a wa al-Lugha al-Arabia wa Adabiha,* p. 526.

[52] Israel Ben Zeev (Abu Zuaib), *Ka'ab al-Ahbar,* pp. 36-37; see also Karen Armstrong, *A History of Jerusalem: One City, Three Faiths,* p. 230.

[53] Moshe Gil, *A History of Palestine: 634-1099,* p. 71.

[54] Patricia Crone and Michael Cook (1977), *Hagarism: the Making of the Islamic World* (Cambridge University Press), p. 156.

[55] Shlomo D. Goitein (1982), 'Jerusalem in the Arab period: 638-1099', *The Jerusalem Cathedra,* 2, pp. 171-172. Karen Armstrong, in her anonymous referee's report on this article, commented on Goitein's claim 'that the Jews had acted as guides around the City' by saying that 'I have never seen this argued'. She argues that 'Jews certainly helped the Muslim army as scouts in the countryside of Palestine, but it was the Christian patriarch who showed Umar around Aelia. But the story that Umar brought rabbis with him from Tiberias may have some historical relevance, even if not literally true. These rabbis were not brought to show the Muslims around the *Bayt al-Maqdis,* the city, but to act as consultants about the reconsecration of the Holy Place ...'

56   John Wilkinson (1989), 'Jerusalem under Rome and Byzantium: 63
      BC - 637 AD' in K.J. Asali (ed.), *Jerusalem in History* (Scorpion
      Publishing, Essex), p. 75.
57   Ibid., p. 88.
58   Aelia (40 square miles) contained: the districts of Gophna,
      Herodium and the area west of Jerusalem which was called Oreine
      or 'Hill Country'. See figure 5 in Ibid, p. 89; see also Muhammad al-
      Maqdisi (1977), *Ahsan al-Taqasim fi Ma'rifat al-Aqalim*, (Baghdad), p.
      173. John Wilkinson argues that 'the area called Jerusalem in Aelia
      Capitolina was thus a very small city', see p. 90.
59   Karen Armstrong 'Sacred Space: the Holiness of Islamic Jerusalem',
      p. 5.
60   See the manuscript in Israel Ben Zeev (Abu Zuaib), *Ka'ab al-Ahbar*,
      p. 39; see also Karen Armstrong, *A History of Jerusalem: One City,
      Three Faiths*, p. 233. Moshe Gil stated that 'Cairo Geniza documents
      occupy first place among Jewish sources, for these were written by
      contemporaries of the period'. Moshe Gil, *A History of Palestine: 634-
      1099*, p. 70.
61   Mustafa A. Hiyari (1989), 'Crusader Jerusalem: 1099 - 1187 AD" in
      K.J. Asali (ed.), *Jerusalem in History* (Scorpion Publishing, Essex), pp.
      131-132. As a result of Fatimid-Byzantium's conflict, al-Hakim in
      1009 CE, for example, ordered his governor of Palestine to destroy
      the Church of the Holy Sepulchre in Jerusalem.
62   Fred McGraw Donner (1981), *The Early Islamic Conquests* (Princeton
      University Press, New Jersey), pp. 322, 287-289; see also Moshe Gil,
      A History of Palestine: 634-1099, p. 71.
63   Neubauer, Aus der Peterburger Bibliothek, 109 VII, p. 12 cited by
      Israel Ben Zeev (Abu Zuaib), *Ka'ab al-Ahbar*, p. 40.
64   J. Mann, *The Jews in Egypt and Palestine under the Fatimid Caliphs*, pp.
      43-47: Muir, *Annals of the Early Califate*, p. 212; Dubnow, *Geschichte
      des judischen Volkes*, III, p. 410 cited by Israel Ben Zeev (Abu Zuaib),
      Ka'ab al-Ahbar, pp. 37-38; see also Moshe Gil, *A History of Palestine:
      634-1099*, p. 71.
65   Schwabe's 'Al-yahud wa al-Haram ba'd al-Fath al-Umari' *Zion Journal*
      (vol. 2), p. 102 cited by Israel Ben Zeev (Abu Zuaib), *Ka'ab al-Ahbar*,
      p. 38.
66   Arculf, *Eines Pilgers Reise nach dem Heiligen Land um 670 aus dem
      lateinischen ubersetzt und erklart von paul mickley* (Leipzig, 1917), p. 29-
      31 cited by Israel Ben Zeev (Abu Zuaib), *Ka'ab al-Ahbar*, p. 38.
67   Israel Ben Zeev (Abu Zuaib), *Ka'ab al-Ahbar*, p. 40.

68 Shafiq Jasir (1999), 'Al-Taghayyurat al-Diymughrafiyah fi al-Quds Abra Tarikhuha' in Shafiq Jasir (ed.), *Jerusalem fi al-Khitab al-Mu'asir* (Jordan), pp. 337-338; see also Moshe Gil, A *History of Palestine: 634-1099*, pp. 71- 72; see also Karen Armstrong, *A History of Jerusalem: One City, Three Faiths*, p. 233.

69 Karen Armstrong's communication with the *Journal of Islamicjerusalem Studies*.

70 Mustafa A. Hiyari 'Crusader Jerusalem: 1099 - 1187 AD', p. 170. During the Latin period only a few Jews lived in Jerusalem near the Citadel. Salah al-Din's tolerant policy allowed the Jews to return to the City. Accordingly, they gradually began to constitute a community. According to J. Prawer, three groups settled this time in Jerusalem, two were Jewish: the Jews from Morocco who fled to the East around 1198-1199, and the Jews from France - some three hundred families - who migrated in two groups in 1210. When Jerusalem was handed over to Frederick II in 1229 anti-Jewish legislation of the Crusaders was re-established and all Jews were again prohibited from living in the city. J. Prawer (1964), 'Minorities in the Crusader states' in *A History of the Crusades* (New York), v, p. 97; Steven Ranciman (1965), *A History of the Crusades* (London), I, p. 467; Karen Armstrong, *A History of Jerusalem: One City, Three Faiths*, pp. 298-299.

71 Donald P. Little (1989), 'Jerusalem under the Ayyubids and Mamluks' in K. J. Asali (ed.), *Jerusalem in History* (Scorpion Publishing, Essex), p. 195.

72 Joseph Drory (1981), 'Jerusalem during the Mamluk period: 1250 – 1517', *The Jerusalem Cathedra*, p. 213.

73 Donald Little (1985), 'Haram Documents related to the Jews of late fourteenth century Jerusalem', *Journal of Semitic Studies* (vol. 30, no. 2, 1985), pp. 227-264.

74 Hani Abu al-Rub, *Tarikh Filastin fi sadr al-Islam*, p. 139.

75 Ibid., p. 214.

76 Ibid., pp. 139, 214.

77 Abd Allah al-Sharif 'Mawqif Yahud al-Sham min al-Fatih al-Islami', p. 513.

78 Ibid., p. 513.

79 Ibid., p. 514.

80 Zakariyya al-Quda, 'Mu'ahadit Fatih Bayt al-Maqdis: al-Uhda al-Umariyya', p. 276

81   The author read this text for the first time in the Arabic language in
      Arif al-Arif (1961), *Al-Mufassal fi Tarikh al-Quds*, (al-Andalus Library,
      Jerusalem), p. 91. This text in Arabic inspired the author to study it
      as al-Arif had done, but using historical technical examination as is
      well known in the historical methodology.

82   Maher Abu-Munshar, *A historical study of Muslim treatment of Christians
      in Islamicjerusalem at the time of Umar Ibn al-Khattab and Salah al-Din with
      special reference to the Islamic value of justice*, pp. 154-155.

83   Asad Rustum (1939), *Mustalah al-Tarikh* (Beirut), pp. 13-20.

84   Abd Allah al-Bakiri al-Andalusiy (1947), *Mu'jam ma Istu'jim* (Cairo),
      part one, p. 217; see also Shafiq Jasir (1989), *Tarikh al-Quds*
      (Amman), p. 19.

85   Ibn Kathir (1978), *Al-Bidayah wa al-Nihayyah* (Beirut), part seven, p.
      55.

86   K.J. Asali (1989), 'Jerusalem under the Ottomans: 1516-1831 AD' in
      K.J. Asali (ed.), *Jerusalem in History* (Scorpion Publishing, Essex), pp.
      206, 210, 221.

87   Maher Abu-Munshar, *A historical study of Muslim treatment of Christians
      in Islamicjerusalem at the time of Umar Ibn al-Khattab and Salah al-Din with
      special reference to the Islamic value of justice*, pp. 158-159.

88   Philip Hitti (1957), *Tarikh al-Arab* (Beirut), part three, pp. 19- 20.

89   A.S. Tritton (1930), *The Caliphs and their non-Muslim Subjects* (Oxford),
      p. 12.

90   Shlomo D. Goitein 'Jerusalem in the Arab period: 638-:1099', p.
      171.

91   Ibid., p. 171.

92   Moshe Gil added that its 'language' and 'its details appear authentic
      and reliable and in keeping with what is known of Jerusalem at that
      time'. Moshe Gil, A *History of Palestine: 634-1099*, p. 56.

93   Ibn Asakir (1329 - 1332 AH), *Tarikh Madinat Dinashq* (Damascus),
      part one, pp. 563-564, 566-567.

94   Mujir al-Din al-'Ulaimi, *Al-Uns al-Jalil hi tarikh al-Quds wa al-Khalil*,
      part one, pp. 253-254.

95   For example, Haroun al-Rashid ordered in 191 AH that non-
      Muslims in areas near the Byzantine frontiers should have a
      different form of address from those of Muslims for security
      reasons. See Ibn al-Athir (1982), *Al-Kamil fi al-Tarikh* (Beirut), part
      six, p. 206.

96   Abdul Aziz Duri, 'Jerusalem in the Early Islamic period: 7th - 11th
      centuries AD', p. 107.

[97] Daniel J. Sahas, 'Patriarch Sophronious, Umar Ibn al-Khattab and the Conquest of Jerusalem', p. 54.

[98] Ibid., p. 60. Karen Armstrong argues that 'The societies that have lasted the longest in the holy city have, generally, been the ones that were prepared for some kind of tolerance and co-existence in the holy city'; and 'the Muslims got their city back because the Crusaders became trapped in a dream of hatred and intolerance.' Karen Armstrong, *A History of Jerusalem: One City, Three Faiths*, pp. 426-427.

[99] Karen Armstrong 'Sacred Space: the Holiness of Islamicjerusalem', pp. 14, 18-19.

[100] Karen Armstrong argues that 'On two occasions in the past, it was an Islamic conquest of Jerusalem that made it possible for Jews to return to their holy City. Umar and Salah al-Din both invited Jews to settle in Jerusalem when they replaced Christian rulers there.' See Karen Armstrong, *A History of Jerusalem: One City, Three Faiths*, p.420; for the same view, see Amnon Cohen (1984), *Jewish life under Islam: Jerusalem in the sixteenth century* (Harvard University Press), p. 14.

5

ISLAMICJERUSALEM AS A MODEL FOR CONFLICT RESOLUTION: A MUSLIM THEORETICAL FRAME OF REFERENCE TOWARDS OTHERS

In the last five years the world has witnessed much debate on new forms of the global phenomena of fundamentalism and extremism. People are more aware of the intense political climate, clashes that have come to be known as 'fundamentalism' or 'extremism'. What these terms mean exactly has yet to be defined, but it is the author's view that at the root of such phenomena lies the disease of ignorance.

It is clear that many view Muslims as 'the other' and vice-versa: an attitude of 'us and them', 'our community and their community'. The concept of a 'clash of civilisations' has become part of our everyday vocabulary. However, the basis of any such clash is either sheer ignorance or an extreme interpretation of the religious scriptures or secular ideologies on which people found their beliefs and actions. Whichever way one looks at it, the author argues strongly that better understanding through education is the solution that will help humankind to break free of the chains of ignorance and rise above extremism. Indeed, education is the most essential way to beat extremists, and to achieve mutual respect and peaceful co-existence. This is a challenge to all communities who should be able to respect one another's differences and have a common ground and a shared purpose. In this context, there is a general need to present how Muslims view others.

Moreover, on the basis of the current conflict in the region, one can define Islamicjerusalem's history more in terms of conflict and exclusion than a common open place for peaceful co-existence. However, the aim of this chapter is to present Islamicjerusalem as a model for conflict resolution. Based on the core Muslim sources, the main key elements of such a model are: the methodological approach of *Tadafu'* (counteraction) and the concept of *'Adl* (Justice), the principle of non-exclusion, and the constructive argumentation methodology.

The main principles for the Muslim theoretical frame of reference towards dealing with others are based on the core Muslim sources, the Qur'an and Sunnah. It was mainly on these sources that the Muslims developed their conceptual and theoretical framework towards non-Muslims. This chapter discusses this frame of reference. To understand this, particular attention will be paid to specific subjects on the Muslim treatment of non-Muslims and the relationship between Muslims and other communities.

Tadafu' methodology

Muslim core teachings reject the philosophy of a conflict based on eliminating the other party so that the victor can have the stage to himself. This would mean in effect annulling the principle of plurality and diversity. As discussed in chapter six, Islam considers that plurality is the basis of everything apart from God. Indeed plurality in nations, religions and religious laws is part of the design of the universe. As confirmation of that idea, Islam favoured another method, namely *Tadafu'* or counteraction, as a means of adjusting positions using movement instead of conflict. For example, one verse of the Qur'an orders Muslims to be patient at the time of anger and to counteract those who treat them badly:

Wa la tastawi al-hasanatu wa la al-sayyi'ah, idfa' bi al-lati hiya ahsanu fa idhal-ladhi baynaka wa baynahu adawatun ka annahu waliyyun hamim. Wa ma yulaqqahaa ill al-ladhina sabaru wa ma yulaqqahaa illa dhu hazzin azim.

The good deed and the evil deed cannot be equal. Counteract the thou (evil) with what is better, and then the one, between whom and thyself there was enmity (will then become) as close as an old and valued friend. Yet (to achieve this quality) this is not granted to anyone but only those who are steadfast in patience and self-restraint – it is not granted to any but only those endowed with the greatest good fortune (Qur'an, 41: 34-35).

This conflict-free method is what Muslim teachings see as a means of preserving a non-Muslim presence in this life. *Tadafu'* is not only to preserve Muslim's sacred places, but to preserve the sacred places of others, mentioned in the following Qur'anic verse about the chronology of religions:

> *Wa lawla daf'u Allah al-nasa ba'dahum bi ba'din lahuddimat sawami'u wa biya'un wa salawatun wa masajidu yudhkaru fiha ismu Allah kathiran*
> ... if God had not counteracted (*Daf'u*) some people by means of others, there would surely have been pulled down monasteries, churches, synagogues, and mosques, wherein the name of God is commemorated in abundant measure (Qur'an, 22: 40).

This means that, from a Muslim point of view, *Tadafu'* is the means of preserving a plurality of sacred places or the plurality of religions.

Concept of *'Adl* (justice)

This methodology is linked to a very central concept in the core Muslim sources, the concept of 'Adl or justice which encompasses all without discriminating between Muslim and non-Muslim. For example, the Qur'an states:

> *Wa la yajrimannakum shana'anu qawmin 'alla an la ta'dilu. 'idilu huwa 'aqrabu li al-taqwa.*
> ... and do not let the enmity and hatred of some people lead you away from justice, but adhere to justice, for that is closer to piety (Qur'an, 5: 8).

The command to be just in this Qur'anic verse is general without specifying any race or group above another. The Prophet Muhammad warned against any unjust action by using a very clear and strong instruction to Muslims that they must deal with non-Muslims justly. He said, 'He who hurts a Dhimi [non-Muslim] hurts me, and he who hurts me hurts Allah.' It is interesting to note here the argument of Ibn al-Qayyim al-Jawziyyah: 'Justice is the supreme goal and objective of Islam ... Any path that leads to justice is an integral part of the religion and can never be against it.'[1]

The Principle of non-exclusion

The claims that Muslims adopt the principle of excluding others from living with them, as discussed in the case of Jews barred from residence in Islamicjerusalem during the first Muslim *Fatih*, has not only not been historically proven, but also contradicts the core Muslim teachings which reject the notion of supremacy of one people or race over others. It contravenes the most basic Islamic principles concerning treatment of the People of the Book. Indeed, the reference in particular to the Jews is out of step, and even seems to clash with the main Muslim teachings, based on the Qur'an and Sunnah. For example, the Qur'an states that the treatment of non-Muslims should be based on fair treatment, kind and good relationships, and justice:

> God does not forbid you to deal kindly and justly (*tabarruhum wa tuqsituu ilayhim*) with those who have not fought you for your faith or driven you out of your homes. God loves those who act equitably (*muqsitin*). But God (only) forbids you to take as allies (*tawallawhum*) those who have fought against you for your faith, driven you out of your homes, and helped others in drive you out; any of you who take them as allies (*man yatawallahum*) will truly be wrongdoers (*al-zalimun*). (Qur'an: 60/8-9)

A young scholar, Abu-Munshar, has examined several interpretations of this verse and presented a very interesting argument. He argues that the terminology *Tabarruhum* means not only to be kind to non-Muslims but to raise their treatment to the level of how one treats one's parent, with *Birr* (love and compassion). In addition, the terminology *Tuqsitn* includes providing non-Muslims with financial support.[2]

As for the issue of the Jews; they were not at the time of the first Muslim *Fatih* at any stage of war with the Muslims in Islamicjerusalem or in any part of the world. As such, how could Umar exclude them from living in Islamicjerusalem? Although at the dawn of Islam, Muslims had had conflicts with the Jewish tribes in and around Madinah and later in Khaibar, they got along very well at all times afterwards, and especially in Islamicjerusalem. In his attempt to discover the reasons behind the contemporary conflict between Muslims and Zionists, the Muslim Jurist, Yusuf al-Qaradawi, argues that 'Muslims did not fight Jews because they are Jews, but because they occupied the Islamic (Muslim) land in Palestine.'[3]

Constructive argumentation methodology

One can argue that the best possible way of resolving a dispute in general and an intellectual disagreement or competing claims in particular between two conflicting parties should be through fair discussion. The Qur'an encourages Muslims to engage in discussion with all people in general and with the People of the Book in particular, through constructive argumentation: 'argue with them *bi-alati hia Ahsanin* in the most beautiful (politest) manner' (Qur'an, 16: 125). The Qur'an lays down one condition for this constructive argumentation methodology, namely, that it should not be only in a beautiful way but in the 'most beautiful manner'.

According to the Qur'an, the starting point for any conflict resolution should be through constructive argumentation based on the power of knowledge and not from an arrogant position. In addition, constructive argumentation is a methodology encouraged by the Qur'an as a means for "constructive dialogue' and positive negotiation with others. Hussien Abdul-Raof, a scholar in Qur'anic studies, argues that 'From a Qur'anic perspective, to argue is to negotiate an opinion; therefore, argumentation is a form of a constructive dialogue whether with an ally or an opponent.' He clarifies his argument, adding that "To argue means to express an opinion with logical and substantiating reasons for or against something with the aim of persuading someone who can be an ally or an opponent in order to share one's own viewpoint.'[4]

Interestingly, from his examination of the Qur'an from a textual linguistics point of view, Abdul-Raof presents two patterns of Qur'anic argumentations, 'thorough-argumentation' and 'counter-argumentation'. In the first pattern 'A thesis is presented which represents its own viewpoint, followed by substantiation which introduces statements to validate the thesis, then a conclusion which supports the thesis and acts as a future back-up for the substantiation part of the argument.' In the second pattern 'A thesis is presented which represents an opponent's viewpoint, followed by opposition which introduces a counter-claim which are statements substantiating its own points of view, then a conclusion which presents a concluding statement that backs-up the opposition part.'[5]

Outcomes: Peaceful Co-Existence and Mutual Respect

The other Muslim core teaching sources conform to this methodology of *Tadafu'*, the concept of *'Adl*, the principle of not excluding others, and the constructive argumentation methodology. Both methodologies, concept, and principles emphasise the need to care for preserving human dignity and belongings. Preserving human dignity is very central in Muslim thoughts and attitude. In a very explicit and sharp manner, Umar asked his governor of Egypt, Amr Ibn al-Aas:

> *Mata Ista'batum al-Nas wa qad Waladathum Umahatuhum Ahraran?*
> How could you have enslaved people, when their mothers have born them free?[6]

This very important international declaration was made by Umar when he received a complaint from an Egyptian Coptic man who was hit by Muhammad, the son of Amr Ibn al-Aas, who claimed to be 'the son of honoured people'. Umar called both Amr, his son, and the Coptic man to Madinah where he asked the Coptic man to hit Amr's son back in public, which he did.

One can argue that this preservation leads to the establishment of tolerance and the elimination of fear and worries resulting from forcing people to change their religion '*laa ikraha fi al-din*, there is no compulsion in religion'. (Qur'an, 2: 256) The principle of tolerance not only means rejecting the notion of compulsion in religions and cultures but promoting the appreciation and acceptance of others. This should lead not only to respect for non-Muslim rights but to granting them protection of lives and properties, freedom, security and support, and enabling them to become citizens and members of the society without interference in their culture and religion. Determining the status and rights of non-Muslims should act as a means to a peaceful co-existence and mutual respect among the different cultures and religions in a society. In this way, Ahmad al-Sharif argues, the ideal Muslim community is 'an open community, where all human beings could live together on the basis of equality and justice'[7]. Muhammad Said al-Buti, a leading Muslim jurist, argues that:

> The Muslim state is not a monopoly of the Muslims alone ... The Muslim system of statehood has a religious concept which the Muslims have to deal with and implement, just as it has an organisational legal concept which encompasses Muslims and non-Muslims. Each group interacts with it according to its status, either from a religious basis stemming from belief in Islam and its tenets, or from a social, legal standpoint based on law and order[8].

The first Muslim state implemented this concept clearly in its domestic and foreign dealings with non-Muslims. On the domestic front, for example, Prophet Muhammad wrote a document known as *al-Sahifah* 'The Constitution of Madinah', in which he laid down the basis of relations with the Jews who lived in the bosom of the Islamic state. On the foreign front, there are examples in the contract that he concluded with the Magian people of Bahrain and the contract that he concluded with the Christian inhabitants of Najran. According to Muhammad Ibn Sa'd (died 232AH/845CE), when the Najran Christian delegation came to al-Madinah, the Prophet not only welcomed them in his Mosque but allowed them to say their prayers there. During their visit, they used to pray in one part of the Prophet's Mosque while the Muslims performed their prayer in another part.[9]

What some early Muslim jurists subsequently wrote about dealing with the People of the Book indeed undermined the frame of reference and the vision of Islamicjerusalem. On the other hand, prominent Muslim jurists in particular, al-Nawawi in his book *Rawdat al-Talibin* (126-215/10), Ibn Qudama in his book *Al-Mughni* (358-357/9), and Abu Ubayd in his book *Kitab Al-Amwal,* have strictly rejected and warned against adopting the ruling which undermined the status of non-Muslims. Among the contemporary leading Muslim jurists who have written on the subject is al-Buti, who also agrees that the early rejected Muslim jurists' view "conflicts vehemently with the guidance of the Messenger of God in his words and deeds, just as it conflicts with what the righteous followers did, and with the piety with which God ordered the Muslims to behave towards the People of the Book in the Qur'an"[10]. The author is inclined to argue that the contraventions, additions, or interpretations invented by some Muslim jurists were produced to please the rulers or match the general circumstances and socio-political developments that affected the position of the People of the Book during certain periods of history, especially the Abbasid state.

Islamicjerusalem as a Model for Conflict Resolution

The best practical and clear model to represent this policy of dealing with non-Muslims is Umar's Assurance of Safety to the people of Aelia. Indeed, his Assurance is the major religious pillar and the frame of reference to establish the nature of this relationship between the communities of Islamicjerusalem's society, which rejects the notion of the supremacy of one people or race over others.

Perhaps all these elements is what prompted Salah al-Din's letter of reply to King Richard I 'the Lionheart' of England in October 1191 CE during the negotiations in the third Crusade. In an exclusive agenda, Richard claimed that 'Jerusalem is the centre of our worship, which we shall never renounce, even if there is only one of us left.' Salah al-Din replied by stating that Islamicjerusalem is the sacred legacy of the followers of all nations. He asserted the Muslim rights without denying the Christian rights in Islamicjerusalem and refuted Richard's claim that Muslims were invaders. In his reply, he stated that: *'Islamicjerusalem is ours as much as it is yours.* It is even more important for us, since it is the site of our Prophet's Night Journey and the place where the people will assemble on the Day of Judgment. Do not imagine, therefore, that we can waver in this regard.'[11]

Indeed, one good example which represents Islamicjerusalem as a model for conflict resolution were the negotiations between Salah al-Din and King Richard I 'the Lionheart' of England during the third Crusade (1189-1193)[12]. Their constructive dialogues not only led to resolving very complicated competing claims but ended with building confidence and establishing a good relationship and mutual respect between the two great leaders - which in their turn led to secure peace in one of the most conflicted areas. They succeeded in reaching an agreement, Al-Ramla Peace Treaty, which was signed on 23 Sha'ban 588AH/2 September 1192 CE.

According to Ibn Shaddad, during these negotiations, on 9 July 1192 CE Richard sent a message to Salah al-Din, *'The King of England desires your love and friendship.'* He went further by handing Count Henry, Richard's nephew and "his troop over to your authority. If you were to summon them for execution they would hear and obey'. This received a very positive response from Salah al-Din on 11 July, who replied, 'If you make this sort of overture to us, *goodwill cannot be met with other than goodwill.* Your nephew will be to me like one of my sons. You shall hear how I shall treat him.'[13] Later on, when Richard met with Chamberlain al-Hajib Abu Bakr, he told him *'This sultan of yours is a great man. Islam has no greater or mightier prince on earth than him ... By God, he is great.*'[14]

Stanley Lane-Pool argues that 'The secret behind Saladin's [Salah al-Din's] power lay in the love of his subjects. What others sought to attain by fear, by severity, by majesty, he accomplished by kindness.'[15] In his words to one of his sons, Salah al-Din revealed the source of his own strength was to:

> seek to win the hearts of the people, and watch over their prosperity; for it is to secure their happiness … I have become great as I am because I have won men's (people's) hearts by gentleness and kindness[16].

Abu-Munshar concludes his discussion on these negotiations by arguing that, although Salah al-Din was a 'determined fighter and a good strategist', he was a 'model of chivalry; he was generous towards defeated enemies, kind toward the Crusaders' wives and women, and humane with captured prisoners. Once he regained Islamicjerusalem he left it open to pilgrims of all faiths.'[17]

Indeed, one can argue that Islamicjerusalem, which has as one of its main characteristics competing political and religious claims, should be presented as a model for conflict resolution through constructive argumentation methodology as a means for a 'constructive dialogue' and positive negotiation with its conflicting parties. The adopting of this constructive dialogue methodology in the past has opened the way for conflict resolution in the region. The late Michael Prior, a Christian academic theologian activist who was a friend to this project on Islamicjerusalem Studies, argued that 'with such interest shown by each of the three religions, one might expect Jerusalem to be an a ideal place for inter-religious dialogue and sharing.'[18]

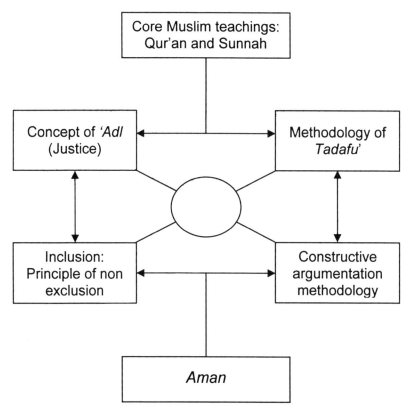

Diagram 2: Islamicjerusalem models for peaceful
co-existence and mutual respect

In conclusion, the question which needs to be asked here is: what is the relationship between these four elements, the methodology of *Tadafu'*, the concept of *'Adl*; the principle of non-exclusion, and the constructive argumentation methodology? As in the case of the definition of Islamicjerusalem, these four principles are intertwined key elements of this model. It is not possible to separate them as not one of them operates without the others. They are also linked and interlinked with their religious context. However, they do not operate simultaneously, with one simply reflecting the others.

In short, one can see from this discussion that Islamicjerusalem is described as a model for conflict resolution which consists of four key interlinked elements. The diagrams which the author presented in the process of constructing these relationships could be used to understand the Muslim theoretical frame of reference towards others.

---

1   Ibn al-Qayyim al-Jawziyyah (n.d.), *Al-Turuq al-Hukmiyyah fi al-Siyasah al-Shar'iyyah* (ed. by Muhammad Jamil Ghazi, Matba'at al-Madaina), p.16.

2   Maher Abu-Munshar (2003), *A historical study of Muslim treatment of Christians in Islamicjerusalem at the time of Umar Ibn al-Khattab and Salah al-Din with special reference to the Islamic value of justice*, pp. 22-28.

3   Yusuf al-Qaradawi 'al-Quds fi al-Wa'yi al-Islami', *Journal of Islamicjerusalem Studies* (no. 1, vol. 1, Winter 1997), pp. 13-14.

4   Hussein Abdul-Raof (2003), *Exploring the Qur'an* (Al-Maktoum Institute Academic Press, Scotland), p. 117.

5   Ibid., p. 119. For more examples on these two patterns of argumentation see pp. 306- 325.

6   "متى استعبدتم الناس وقد ولدتهم امهاتهم احرارا". Abu al-Faraj Abd al-Rahman Ibn Ali Ibn al-Jawzi (ed. 2001), *Sirat wa Manaqb Amir al-Mu'minin Umar Ibn al-Khattab* (ed. by M. Amr, Dar al-Da'wah al-Islamiyyah, Cairo), p. 89.

7   Ahmad al-Sharif (1976), *Dirast fl al-Hadarah al-Islamiyyah* (Cairo), p. 123.

8   Muhammad Said al-Buti 'Mu'amalit al-Dawlah al-Islamiyyah li ghaiyr al-Muslimin: al-Quds Namwudhajan', *Journal of Islamicjerusalem Studies* (no. 1, vol. 3, Winter 1999), pp. 3-4.

9   Muhammad Ibn Sa'd, *Al-Tabaqat al-Kubra* (Beirut, 1985), vol. 1, p. 358.

10 Muhammad Said al-Buti 'Mu'amalit al-Dawlah al-Islamiyyah li ghaiyr al-Muslimin: al-Quds Namwudhjan', p. 10.

11 Baha' al-Din Ibn Shaddad, *Al-Nawadir al-Sultaniyya wa al-Mahsin al-Yusufiyya* (Cairo, 1964), III, p. 265; see also Donald P. Little 'Jerusalem under the Ayyubids and Mamluks', p. 179.

12 The author gave Ramona Ahmed Ibrahim, one of the taught Master's students in Islamic Jerusalem Studies, a draft copy of this chapter (before it was finalised) and encouraged her to conduct her Master's dissertation on Islamicjerusalem as a Model of Conflict Resolution: a Case Study of the Negotiation between Salah al-Din and Richard the Lionheart (1191 – 1192 CE).

13   Emphasis on the quote was made by the author. See Ibn Shaddad, *Al-Nawadir al-Sultaniyya wa al-Mahasin al-Yusufiyyah*, p. 176; and Baha' al-Din Ibn Shaddad, *The rare and excellent history of Saladin*, pp. 213-214; both quoted by Maher Abu-Munshar (2003), *A historical study of Muslim treatment of Christians in Islamicjerusalem at the time of Umar Ibn al-Khattab and Salah al-Din with special reference to the Islamic value of justice*, pp. 248-249.

14   Ibn Shaddad, *Al-Nawadir al-Sultaniyya wa al-Mahasin al-Yusufiyyah*, p. 177 as quoted by Maher Abu-Munshar (2003), *A historical study of Muslim treatment of Christians in Islamicjerusalem at the time of Umar Ibn al-Khattab and Salah al-Din with special reference to the Islamic value of justice*, pp. 250-251.

15   Stanley Lane-Poole (1985), *Saladin and the fall of the Kingdom of Jerusalem* (Dare Publishers, London), p. 367.

16   Ibid., pp. 367-368.

17   Maher Abu-Munshar (2003), *A historical study of Muslim treatment of Christians in Islamicjerusalem at the time of Umar Ibn al-Khattab and Salah al-Din with special reference to the Islamic value of justice*, p. 257; see also pp. 239-256.

18   Michael Prior 'Christian perspectives on Jerusalem', *Journal of Islamicjerusalem Studies*, vol. 3, no.1 (Winter 1999), p. 2.

6

ISLAMICJERUSALEM AS A MODEL FOR MULTICULTURALISM

As discussed earlier, the core Muslim sources consider diversity and plurality to be the basis of everything apart from God. Indeed, diversity and plurality in nations, religions and religious laws is part of the design of the universe. In respect of their cultural, religious, or gender differences, the Qur'an addresses humans and reminds them that they belong to the same family, *ya a'yyuh al-nasu inna khalaqnakum min dhakarin wa untha* 'O humankind! We created you all from a single pair of a male and a female' (Qur'an, 49:13). In addition, Prophet Muhammad is narrated to have said that 'You are all the children of Adam.' In another verse, the Qur'an says *wa law shaa'a Allah laja'alakum ummatan wahidatan* 'If God had so willed, He could surely have made you all human one single community (nation)' (Qur'an, 5: 48). From this point of reference, he 'made you into nations and tribes' *wa ja'alnakum shu'uban wa qabaa'ila*. The main purpose for this creation is *li ta'arafu* 'so that you should get to know one another' (Qur'an, 49:13), not that you may despise one another. On the bases of the Muslim core sources, the Qur'an in particular, the author argues that the first step in establishing a multicultural society is to identify and recognise diversity and plurality.

The unique region of Islamicjerusalem can be argued as the model place where this one family can live together. Accordingly, instead of examining the views of Islam and Muslims on diversity and plurality or their understanding of multiculturalism, the aim of this chapter is to present Islamicjerusalem as a model for multiculturalism. In addition, it highlights Shaikh Hamdan Bin

Rashid Al-Maktoum's vision which is based on the understanding of Islamicjerusalem as a model for multiculturalism.

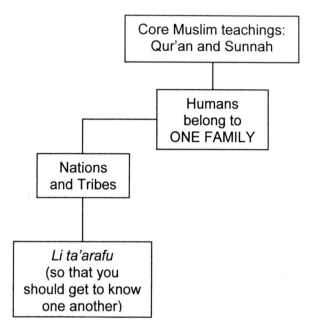

Diagram 3: Islamicjerusalem models for peaceful co-existence and mutual respect

The Vision

The first Muslim *Fatih* of Islamicjerusalem was a fundamental landmark which reshaped relations between the people of diverse faiths and cultures who inhabited the region. The arrival of Umar Ibn al-Khattab (d 24 AH/645 CE) in the region marked the beginning of a new and distinguished phase in the relations between the followers of the three great Semitic religions, Judaism, Christianity, and Islam. Instead of continuing to implement the Byzantines' exclusion policy, Umar, as head of the Muslim state, not only rejected the idea of excluding others who would like to live in the region, he was categorically pro-active in establishing a new policy and system. Karen Armstrong argues that 'The Muslims had established a system that enabled Jews, Christians, and Muslims to live in Jerusalem together for the first time.'[1]

The arrival of Umar in the region also marked the start of a golden age and the beginning of a new era in which Islamicjerusalem became a common and open space for everyone and a model for multiculturalism. This model was based not only on fostering the culture of diversity, plurality and mutual respect and implementing tolerance and recognition of others, but on determining their rights, duties, and treatment as a means to encourage and establish a peaceful co-existence between the different communities in Islamicjerusalem.

Umar's model for a multicultural Islamicjerusalem was based on the core Muslim teachings, the Qur'an and Sunnah. Moreover, the methodology of *Tadafu'*, the concept of *'Adl*, and the principle of non-exclusion, together not only emphasise the recognition of others but also took great care to preserve the dignity of humans and what belonged to them as prescribed in the Muslim core teaching sources. As discussed earlier, preserving human dignity is a very central issue in Muslim thought and attitude. The explicit and sharp declaration of Umar to his governor of Egypt, Amr Ibn al-Aas, that 'how could you have enslaved people, when their mothers have born them free'[2], is a very clear example of this.

One may argue that this understanding and attitude to preserving human dignity and the recognition of others led Umar to implement the principles of tolerance and mutual respect. On his Assurance to the people of Aelia, Umar laid down the foundation of fostering diversity and plurality in Islamicjerusalem. Not only did he recognise and appreciate others' presence in Islamicjerusalem, he accepted them and offered a framework which demonstrated that it could be shared with them. Indeed, he not only also respected non-Muslim rights but, as shown in chapter four, he took practical steps to grant them protection, safety and security for their rights, lives and properties. He granted them freedom, and enabled them to become citizens and members of the society, without interference in their culture and religious life. In short, Umar not only identified, he also accommodated, the presence and needs of his diverse citizens and established a system to protect their rich cultural diversity, identities and belongings. By establishing this model, one can argue that Umar's aim was to preserve the human dignity of the people of Islamicjerusalem in status and rights regardless of their culture, religion, race and gender. This clearly manifested itself in the personal liberty, freedom and equality granted to the people of Islamicjerusalem in Umar's Assurance of Safety.

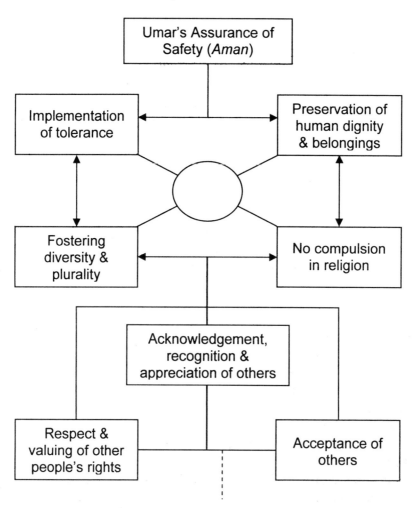

Diagram 4: Islamicjerusalem models for peaceful co-existence and mutual respect

Leading to:

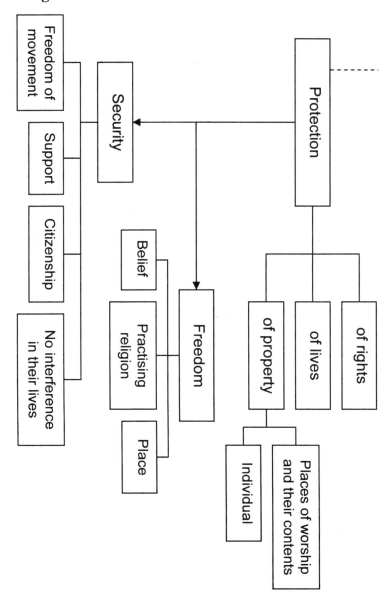

Diagram 5: Islamicjerusalem models for peaceful
co-existence and mutual respect

One of the most important elements for this model's success was how the state and its established power and authority managed the diverse society of Islamicjerusalem. The foundations for managing the future relations between the three faiths were laid down during that historical visit in the form of what is known in history as Al-Uhda al-Umariyya or Umar's Assurance of Safety to the people of Aelia, as discussed in chapter four. Although this was a practical application of the core Muslim teachings, the Qur'an and Sunnah, it was the major outcome of the first Muslim *Fatih* of Aelia. Indeed, it was the practical management initiative to implement the new vision. In addition, it formed the cornerstone to manage and implement the new vision where Umar granted the people of Aelia an Assurance of Safety for themselves, their property, their churches, and their religion. Indeed, Umar's Assurance of Safety is an important reference text and a theoretical framework which laid down the foundation principles and the essential criteria to establish and manage a multicultural society in Islamicjerusalem for the first time. It introduced, defined, and legislated the status and rights of non-Muslims in Islamicjerusalem and ensured a peaceful co-existence between the different communities there.

On this basis, Umar not only implemented this theoretical framework but demonstrated his protection practically during his first visit to Islamicjerusalem. Among the early events during this visit, which emphasised his keenness to protect non-Muslim holy places, was Umar's refusal to pray either in the Church of the Holy Sepulchre or its atrium when he was visiting the place and was invited to do so by Patriarch Sophronious. Abu-Munshar quoting Eutychius, Sa'id Ibn al-Batriq, reconstructed the recording of the conversation between Umar and Patriarch. Umar's justification for his refusal was

> If I prayed inside the Church, it would have been lost by you and would have slipped from your power; for after my death the Muslims would take it away from you, together saying that 'Umar prayed here[3].

According to this account, it seems that Umar was not satisfied that his verbal explanation might be enough to convince the Muslims following his death not to change the church into a mosque. Umar wrote Sophronious a decree which read, 'The Muslims shall not pray on the stairs, unless it be one person at a time. But, they shall not meet there for a congregational prayer announced by the prayer call.'[4]

Moreover, Umar also succeeded during his visit in establishing mutual respect with the Islamicjerusalem people. Sophronious trusted Umar with the Christians' holiest shrine when he entrusted him with the keys of the Church of the Holy Sepulchre. In addition to establishing this mutual respect, Sophronious secured the protection of the Church from Christian-Christian dispute. According to this account, Umar passed the keys to one of his companions, Abd Allah Ibn Nusaibah[5].

All the changes introduced by Umar were essential steps towards implementing this new vision, policy and system. However, certain aspects relating to Islamicjerusalem were not altered. For example, the name was unchanged, as research showed earlier, and neither were its geographical boundaries. Also this area was not chosen as the capital. In addition, there was no thought of making Muslims the majority in Islamicjerusalem. Karen Armstrong argues that Muslims were the minority in Islamicjerusalem until the Crusader period[6]. A young Malaysian postgraduate student, Fatimatulzahra Abd al-Rahman, examined Armstrong's argument and presented an interesting discussion which concluded that this was the case.[7] One can argue that the main issue for Muslims at that time was not to change its demographical population by excluding non-Muslims and transferring Muslims from Arabia to settle in Islamicjerusalem so they would become the majority. Indeed, this matter highlights the unique nature of a multicultural Islamicjerusalem where the subject of majority and minority was not the issue. The main concern was to establish a new vision for Islamicjerusalem, which would lead to a peaceful co-existence and mutual respect between the different communities in the region.

The author argues that what prevented Muslims from doing all this was their vision of Islamicjerusalem. If Makkah and Madinah were exclusive cities for Muslims, Islamicjerusalem was made by Muslims into an inclusive, multi-religious, and multicultural region where all traditions and cultures could live in peace and harmony. According to one verse in the Qura'an, Islamicjerusalem is 'the land which We have given *Barakah* **for everyone in the universe'** (Qur'an 21:71). This is the main vision of Islamicjerusalem – an inclusive not an exclusive one. Karen Armstrong argues that Umar Ibn al-Khattab was 'faithful to the Islamic inclusive vision. Unlike the Jews and Christians, Muslims did not attempt to exclude others from (Islamic) Jerusalem's holiness'[8] and, instead of excluding these religions, 'Muslims were being taught to venerate them'[9]. In addition, Armstrong argues that:

> From the first, Muslims showed that the veneration of sacred space did not have to mean conflict, enmity, killing … and exclusion of others … From the start, the Muslims developed an inclusive vision of [Islamic] Jerusalem which did not deny the presence and devotion of others, but respected their rights and celebrated plurality and co-existence. This inclusive vision of holiness is sorely needed by the people of [Islamic] Jerusalem today[10].

Islamicjerusalem represents for Muslims a region of hope, peace and stability. As discussed earlier, it was the region of hope for Prophet Abraham. When his people in his home country tried to kill him, he was ordered to migrate to the land of hope, Islamicjerusalem. Once again, when Prophet Muhammad lost hope of any support in Makkah and the surrounding area, he was taken by night to the land of hope, Islamicjerusalem. Since then, Islamicjerusalem has always been a symbol of hope for Muslims. Even with all the turmoil and troubles in the region, it still represents for contemporary Muslims the land of hope for the future.

The first Muslim *Fatih* of Islamicjerusalem put an end to centuries of instability, religious exclusion, persecution and colonial rule. When Muslims came to Islamicjerusalem, the first thing they did was to solve the existing religious and social problems by establishing peace between the inhabitants of that region. Before the first Muslim *Fatih*, Aelia had been a closed and insular region, mainly for Byzantine Christians. Indeed, it was very much an exclusive region, i.e. just for the locals and the Byzantines. Islamicjerusalem, on the other hand, was not an exclusive region during Muslim rule but an inclusive one. For example, Jews returned to Islamicjerusalem only when the Muslims took over and opened it up to all nations. The Jews had been excluded by the Romans (Hadrian) in 135 AD, but the Muslims brought them back after 500 years to establish peace between the three Abrahamic faiths, Islam, Christianity and Judaism. For the first time in history, these three religions managed to live together under the new vision of Islamicjerusalem.

The author argues that the first Muslim *Fatih* liberated the Christians from the persecution of Byzantine occupiers, rid the Jews of Byzantine oppression, restored their presence to that region after an absence of five hundred years[11], enabled all the communities to live side by side peacefully for the first time after a long history of conflict, and provided the grounds for establishing Islamicjerusalem as a model for multiculturalism..

The Christians of Aelia greatly welcomed the first Muslim *Fatih*[12]. This could be argued as being related to the new vision of Islamicjerusalem which provided Christians with the respect which would lead to good treatment, peace, security and stability. Runciman argues that Orthodox Christians "finding themselves spared the persecution that they had feared and paying taxes that, in spite of the *Jizya* demanded from the Christians, were far lower than in the Byzantine times, showed small inclination to question their destiny"[13]. In addition, Runciman quotes Jacobite Patriarch of Antioch, Michael the Syrian, who stated that God 'raised from the south the children of Ishmael (Muslims) to deliver us from the hands of the Romans.'[14] Moreover, Butler quotes Ibn al-Ibri who stated that Christians were optimistic towards the Muslims, 'God of vengeance delivered us out of the hand of the Romans by means of the Arabs. Then although our Churches were not restored to us, since under Arab rule each Christian community retained its actual possession, still it profited us not a little to be saved from the cruelty of the Romans and their bitter hatred against us.' Karen Armstrong argues that it was not surprising that Nestorian and Monophysite Christians welcomed Muslims and found them preferable to the Byzantines[15].

The Muslim sources also record a letter sent to the Muslim army, when Abu Ubayda camped in Fahl in the Jordan Valley: 'O Muslims, we prefer you to the Byzantines, although they are of our own faith, because you keep faith with us and are more merciful to us and refrain from doing us injustice and your rule over us is better than theirs, for they have robbed us of our goods and our homes.'[16]

As discussed in chapter four, Jewish sources show that the Jews of Syria were 'patiently awaiting' the arrival of the Muslim armies because they were groaning under the rule of the tyrannical Byzantines and suffering cruel oppression in the fifth, sixth, and early seventh centuries C.E.[17] The Jewish response to the first Muslim *Fatih* of Islamicjerusalem was 'characterised as generally positive'[18], because it terminated the Byzantine rule and liberated them from their oppressor.

After the re-*Fatih* of Islamicjerusalem by Salah al-Din in 1187, two new quarters were created within the walls of the Old City: the Maghrabi quarter and the Jewish quarter with the Sharaf quarter in between. In short, the Muslim *Fatih* of Islamicjerusalem made it possible for Jews to return to the region. Both Umar and Salah al-Din invited Jews to settle in Islamicjerusalem. When Islam ruled in that part of the world, both after the first Muslim *Fatih* in the time of Umar Ibn Khattab and after the second liberation by Salah al-Din, the different traditions managed to live in harmony and peace with one another.

Crusade historians[19], such as William of Tyre and Michael Foss, argue that for 372 years, since the first Muslim *Fatih* in 637 until 1009 (Al-Hakim ruling), Christians practised their religion freely[20]. Moreover, Islamicjerusalem was for the Christians an open and safe region to travel to[21]. In addition, both Christians and Jews were employed by the Muslim authority in Islamicjerusalem in all positions. Ahmad Ibn Tulun, the local Turkish commander, who established an independent state in Egypt away from the Abbasid Caliphate from 868-904, appointed a Christian as a governor of Islamicjerusalem. He also allowed a new Jewish sect to establish itself in the region[22]. Al-Maqdisi described the situation of both Christians and Jews in Islamicjerusalem before the beginning of the Crusader period: 'Everywhere the Christians and Jews have the upper hand.'[23]

With this peace among the different religions and cultures, stability was the obvious result. The whole region witnessed this very clearly. The author argues that Islamicjerusalem had always held the key to war and peace in the region. Whenever it has been blessed with security and peace, the whole region has enjoyed peace, security and stability. There is no doubt that settling the issue of Islamicjerusalem in a way that ensures justice and restores the rights of its people holds the key to world peace and regional stability. One can argue that, to achieve global peace and stability, it is necessary to have peace and stability in Islamicjerusalem. Until this is achieved the entire world will not rest. Peace and stability in that region would bring about global peace and stability. Indeed, Islamicjerusalem acts as a centre for peace and for conflict in the world. Some might argue that this may be true for the Muslim Arab world but not for the rest of the world. The author argues that the formula is a global one. In the past, why did the farmers leave their land in Europe to go and fight during the Crusader period? Today, for example, when there is a conflict in that region, everyone pays the price of that war in one way or another: more taxes, higher petrol prices, etc.

What was the basis of that original peace and stability? The author argues that it was the concept of 'Adl (justice), as discussed earlier. Justice is a pre-requisite for peace and stability. The formula which has been produced on the peace process negotiations for the current conflict in the Muslim Arab world in the last decade is based on the Arab and the Palestinian point of view of Peace for

Land, and on the Israeli point of view, Peace for Security. The author argues that neither viewpoint is an appropriate formula. The exchange of land will not bring peace and security. In addition, imposing security will not bring peace. For the author, the formula based on his understanding of the history of the region should be that neither peace nor security will be established without justice. So, the formula should be peace for justice which will lead to preserving human dignity and tolerance. In other words, justice is necessary before peace can be achieved.

The Muslim vision for Islamicjerusalem was to establish peace and stability in the area. To achieve this goal, one could argue that sovereignty is necessary. However, it is the Muslim vision of inclusion that is important, and not having sovereignty over the region and its people - although that too is important. However, sovereignty (*Siyadah*) over territory and people does not mean ownership (*Milkiya*) as it does not give the right of the ruling power to confiscate individual ownership of property or to own individuals. As quoted by Aminurraasyid Yatiban, Wahbah al-Zuhayli argues that:

> sovereignty gives the legal power to the state to take any suitable action regarding the land under its authority, such as introducing certain regulations. It does not have the right to abandon the individual ownership of private land, unless to be used for public necessity but also with compatible value of compensation[24].

Indeed, sovereignty only gives power to administer the well-being of the people and safeguard its territory. In short, Umar used his power to reshape a good relationship between the different communities establishing Islamicjerusalem as a model for multiculturalism.

One can argue that sovereignty alone does not lead to peace, security and stability. Without the vision coming first, there will never be peace or security and stability as both the Crusaders and the Israelis have shown. It is the inclusive nature of the vision that allows people to live in peace, even if this is a Muslim vision and those living under the vision are not all Muslims. Generally, during

Muslim rule, people in Islamicjerusalem enjoyed safety, peace, security, stability and prosperity - with the exception of the period of the Crusades (1099-1198). Indeed, Islamicjerusalem enjoyed, in particular, the special care of the Caliphs and the Muslim rulers. In addition to being a spiritual and political centre, Islamicjerusalem was also a cultural, learning and teaching centre from which a large number of scholars graduated. Scholarly activities took place on a wider scale and at various levels, and schools, mosques and hospitals were founded.

In short, Islamicjerusalem was created by Muslims as an inclusive, multi-religious and multicultural region, where all traditions and cultures could live in peace and stability. It is not closed and limited, but a centre in which the richness of cultural diversity and pluralism thrive in a spirit of mutual respect and co-existence. This was the vision of Islamicjerusalem in the past during Muslim rule. Indeed, in this age where we are trying to promote multiculturalism at global level, Islamicjerusalem could serve as the model - giving us, as it does, the model of a common space in which people from different backgrounds can live in peace together.

One can argue that the differences between cultures, communities, and religions should give strength to the society as a whole. Indeed, the different cultural lenses which people from diverse backgrounds bring to their society should enrich their experiences and add to their pursuit for a common ground. In examining Umar's Assurance as a whole, it was seen that Muslims were not afraid of recognising the needs of and dealing with others. On the contrary, they discovered and established a model where they saw how practically fostering a culture of diversity, plurality and mutual respect of differences was positive and a strength rather than a threat.

As well, the Muslims demonstrated that this model could even work in conflict situations and areas where there had been long centuries of war and exclusion. Even at a later stage, Salah al-Din was very faithful and committed to this inclusive vision. As discussed earlier, during the negotiations in the third Crusade, Salah al-Din replied to King Richard I 'the Lionheart' of England in October 1191 CE by acknowledging Christian rights in Islamicjerusalem, asserting Muslim rights and refuting Richard's claim that Muslims were invaders. In his reply, he stated 'Islamicjerusalem is ours as much it is yours.'[25]

Indeed, Umar successfully created, developed and managed a new multicultural environment in Islamicjerusalem where differences among its people were not only acknowledged and recognised but accepted, respected, valued, and protected. Islamicjerusalem provides and promotes a climate of religious and cultural engagement and dialogue, tolerance and diversity, and social justice. It also encourages, supports, and contributes to fostering a multicultural ethos of mutual cultural understanding and respect, and a common understanding between different communities and individuals at all levels.

Shaikh Hamdan Bin Rashid Al-Maktoum's Vision for Multiculturalism[26]

This understanding of Islamicjerusalem has become clearer through the passion and vision of Shaikh Hamdan Bin Rashid Al-Maktoum – Deputy Ruler of Dubai and the UAE Minister for Finance and Industry, particularly through his development and support of education and scholarship. His vision is based on Umar's Assurance of Safety and the central principle of developing the focus of Islamicjerusalem as a key model for multiculturalism, cultural engagement, and mutual understanding and respect.

His actions have established strong foundations for the building and the realisation of this vision. A first step in this process was the establishment of the new field of inquiry of Islamicjerusalem Studies, to which Shaikh Hamdan made a vital contribution. Through his support and encouragement, Islamicjerusalem Studies was pioneered and developed as a field, in particular at Al-Maktoum Institute. It was through his efforts that the Al-Maktoum Institute for Arabic and Islamic Studies was established in 2001 in Dundee, Scotland, the United Kingdom, which was officially opened by HH Shaikh Hamdan on 6 May 2002. In addition, it was through the author's academic research that Islamicjerusalem as a model of multiculturalism has now been understood and established.

Al-Maktoum Institute in Dundee is a unique academic and cultural establishment in the west; it is a new stage for the understanding of Islam and Muslims in the west and a key bridge between the peoples of today's world. The Institute is a living and tangible model of inclusiveness which reflects and demonstrates this vision of Islamicjerusalem.

As a unique development, Al-Maktoum Institute also works to generate an atmosphere in which cultural engagement and dialogue rather than clashes can take place. It works to build bridges between communities at all levels, in particular between people across the world in these crucial times by providing a unique and innovative academic environment and community for learning, teaching and research in the study of Islam and Muslims. This vision helps the Institute to establish its strategic agenda in the study of Islam and Muslims - post-orientalist, post-traditionalist, and multicultural.

The aim of the Institute is to be a centre of excellence in the study of Islam and Muslims, in particular to promote intelligent debate and understanding of Islam and the role of Muslims in the contemporary world, and to be a place of knowledge and reflection on the issues facing a diverse and multicultural world in the twenty-first century. In pursuit of this aim, the Institute is actively engaged in educating the next generation of scholars and leaders – both nationally and internationally – in the study of Islam and Muslims to enable them to face the challenges and opportunities of a diverse and multicultural world.

The Institute's approach is distinctly different from traditional approaches, where the focus has been to study Islam and Muslims from just one limited perspective. Research and teaching at the Institute looks at Islam and Muslims in many different ways, and in many global contexts. This reflects a diversity of teaching and research interests spanning a variety of subject areas and methodological approaches in the study of Islam and Muslims. Indeed, the Institute does not seek to offer Islamic Studies within a single methodology. It offers interdisciplinary and multidisciplinary training in the study of Islam and Muslims within a number of different methodologies, e.g. history, political science, anthropology, sociology, geography, area studies as well as traditional areas in Islamic Studies.

This new agenda for the study of Islam and Muslims globally is fully mapped out in the *Dundee Declaration for the Future Development of the Study of Islam and Muslims*. One feature of the Dundee Declaration is that it makes clear that the current crisis in the contemporary Muslim world is the absence of co-operation between knowledge and power, and that academic research and teaching in the study of Islam and Muslims should be based on a principle of mutual respect in which people of any faith can share together a common intellectual goal.

One of the Institute's aims is to provide a meeting point between the Western and Muslim worlds of learning. Al-Maktoum Institute also believes that academic excellence can be achieved by forging international academic network and scholarship, particularly through working in partnership with other higher education establishments throughout the world, including not only Scotland but also leading universities in the Gulf, the Middle East, Europe and South East Asia.

United Arab Emirates – Scotland relations

Radiating from the vision of Islamicjerusalem is the Institute's practical model for global cross-cultural understanding and co-operation that is bridging Scotland and the United Arab Emirates for example. Since 2001, one of his main focuses has been on the creation of mutually beneficial relationships between the United Arab Emirates and Scotland. The aim is to help promote a two-way traffic for educational, cultural and business links between the

United Arab Emirates and Scotland, as a practical model of co-operation which is beneficial to both parties.

In the last three years (2002–2005), Dubai has provided a number of initial practical steps for co-operation to bridge Scotland with Dubai. In a short space of time the following has been achieved:

- The development of Al-Maktoum Multicultural Centre in Dundee – as a facility for all the communities of the city and the country, and as a model for multiculturalism in Scotland.

- The Sister City agreement between Dubai and Dundee (6 April 2004): Dubai has built a worldwide network of sister cities – twelve in all – in countries such as China, Japan, Australia, Germany, the United States, Switzerland and across the Arab and Muslim countries. Due to the presence of the Institute, Dundee was invited to become a sister city of Dubai; it is the only city in the UK, and is alone among those sister cities in having an Al-Maktoum Institute. This is a tremendous advantage for Scotland. In May 2004, Dundee City Council leader, Jill Shimi, led Dundee City Council's delegation to Dubai First Sister Cities Forum.

- Emirates Airlines' daily direct flight between Dubai and Glasgow, inaugurated on 10 April 2004. This flight has been so successful that Emirates recently announced that it plans to boost the number of seats on this route by more than 50 percent (from 1 October 2005, 278 to 427 seats), less than a year after the introduction of the daily direct service which is, according to Mr Sheppard, Emirates Vice-President for the UK, a 'direct response to increasing demand from Scottish travellers'. This is a great achievement which represents, says Stephen Baxter, Managing Director of Glasgow Airport, a 'real success story... Not just in terms of passenger numbers, but in an economic sense too. This expansion of Emirates represents a major economic boost for Scottish exporters.' This direct link with the major global economic centre of Dubai is a tremendous advantage for Scottish business development with the UAE and, of course, beyond to other potential partners such as India and China.

It is worth noting that Scotland does not have direct air links with many of these countries, but does have direct links with Dubai.

- The commitment to multiculturalism has been shown in particular by the launch of the Shaikh Hamdan Bin Rashid Al-Maktoum Awards for Multicultural Scotland, awarded for the first time on 15 August 2005. The next Awards will be launched in autumn 2007 for 2008.

- A number of higher education links between Scotland and Dubai, including the establishment of the British University in Dubai, the linking of the University of Aberdeen with Zayed University, four summer training schools in multiculturalism and leadership (2003, 2004, 2005, and 2006) at Al-Maktoum Institute in Dundee for female students from the UAE, and the first student delegation from Scotland to an international conference in Dubai in March 2005 on 'Women as Global Leaders' organised by Zayed University. This delegation was led by Wendy Alexander who delivered a keynote speech.

- Three Scottish delegations to the United Arab Emirates (October 2002, December 2003, and April 2004). The aim was to establish business and economic foundations between the two nations. To develop this, Dubai will be sending a trade mission to Scotland including senior representatives from business and education to further explore how this two-way traffic can be developed.

- Al-Maktoum Institute will be hosting in Dundee from 31 May to 2 June 2007 a meeting of the Al-Maktoum Institute International Academic Network Forum. This will bring together students and scholars from a number of its academic partner universities from across the world, to disseminate the new agenda for the Study of Islam and Muslims.

- To enhance Shaikh Hamdan's practical models for multiculturalism, the Al-Maktoum Foundation was established in 2005 in Scotland.

- Al-Maktoum Institute, together with the new Al-Maktoum Foundation in Scotland, is continually striving to implement Shaikh Hamdan's vision to further facilitate the creation of mutually beneficial relationships between the United Arab Emirates and Scotland. There is much to be gained for both Scotland and the United Arab Emirates by the development of academic, business and economic links, and links in the worlds of culture and art, science and technology, medicine and sport.

All these steps come directly from Shaikh Hamdan's vision to follow and implement the model of multicultural Islamicjerusalem. This will enhance greater understanding and appreciation between communities and peoples at all levels across the world in general and the Arab and Muslim worlds and the West in particular.

In conclusion, Islamicjerusalem was created by Muslims as an inclusive, multi-religious, and multicultural region. Indeed, its uniqueness is highlighted through its vision which presents a model for a peaceful co-existence where people from different religious and cultural backgrounds could live together in an environment of multiculturalism and religious and cultural engagement, diversity and tolerance. This was the nature and identity of Islamicjerusalem in the past during Muslim rule. Indeed, in this age more than ever, where we are trying to promote multiculturalism at a global level, Islamicjerusalem could serve as the model.

---

1   See Karen Armstrong, *A History of Jerusalem: One City, Three Faiths*, p. 246; see also, p. 233.
2   Abu al-Faraj Abd al-Rahman Ibn Ali Ibn al-Jawzi (ed. 2001), *Sirat wa Manaqb Amir al-Mu'minin Umar Ibn al-Khattab*, p. 89.
3   Maher Abu-Munshar (2003), *A historical study of Muslim treatment of Christians in Islamicjerusalem at the time of Umar Ibn al-Khattab and Salah al-Din with special reference to the Islamic value of justice*, pp. 169-170.
4   **Ibid., p. 170.**

5   Although this account was not mentioned in any early sources, Abu-Munshar's satisfaction with its authenticity is based on the fact that the keys are still in the hands of the Al-Nusaibah family. See Maher Abu-Munshar (2003), *A historical study of Muslim treatment of Christians in Islamicjerusalem at the time of Umar Ibn al-Khattab and Salah al-Din with special reference to the Islamic value of justice*, pp. 171-173.

6   Karen Armstrong 'Sacred Space: the Holiness of Islamicjerusalem', pp. 14-15.

7   Fatimatulzahra Abd al-Rahman (2004), Political, Social and Religious Changes in Islamicjerusalem from the First Islamic Conquest until the end of Umayyad period (637 to 750CE): An Analytical Study. (Unpublished Master's Dissertation, Al-Maktoum Institute for Arabic and Islamic Studies).

8   Karen Armstrong 'Sacred Space: the Holiness of Islamicjerusalem', p. 14.

9   Ibid., p. 18.

10   Ibid., pp. 18-19.

11   Karen Armstrong, *A History of Jerusalem: One City, Three Faiths*, p.420; for the same view, see Amnon Cohen, *Jewish life under Islam: Jerusalem in the sixteenth century*, p. 14.

12   Maher Abu-Munshar (2003), *A historical study of Muslim treatment of Christians in Islamicjerusalem at the time of Umar Ibn al-Khattab and Salah al-Din with special reference to the Islamic value of justice*, pp. 161- 167.

13   Steven Runciman (1987), A *History of the Crusades*, (Cambridge Academic Press, Cambridge), vol.1, pp. 20-21.

14   Ibid., pp. 20-21.

15   See Karen Armstrong, *A History of Jerusalem: One City, Three Faiths*, p. 232.

16   Muhammad Ibn Abd Allah al-Azdi (1970), *Tarikh Futuh al-Sham* (ed. by A. Amer, Mu'assasat Sijil al-Arab, Cairo), p. 111.

17   Israel Ben Zeev (Abu Zuaib), *Ka'ab al-Ahbar,* p. 35.

18   Abd Allah al-Sharif 'Mawqif Yahud al-Sham min al-Fatih al-Islami', *Majalat Jami'at Umm al-qura li Ulum al-Shari'a wa al-Lugha al-Arabia wa Adabiha*, p. 526.

19   Abu-Munshar presented an interesting discussion of several accounts on how non-Muslims were treated prior to the Crusade. Maher Abu-Munshar (2003), *A historical study of Muslim treatment of Christians in Islamicjerusalem at the time of Umar Ibn al-Khattab and Salah al-Din with special reference to Islamic value of justice*, pp. 190-196.

20 William of Tyre, (trans. 1976), *A history of deeds done beyond the sea*, translated and annotated by E.A. Babcock Octagon Books (New York), vol. 1, pp. 89-93.
21 Michael Foss (2002), *People of the first Crusades*, (Caxton, London), p. 29.
22 Karen Armstrong, *A History of Jerusalem: One City, Three Faiths*, pp. 254-255.
23 Abu Abd Allah Muhammad al-Maqdisi (1909), Ahsan al-Taqasim Fi Ma'rift al-Aqalim, (Brill, Leiden), 2nd edition, p. 167.
24 Wahbah al-Zuhayli (2002), *Al-Fiqh al-Islami wa Adillatuh* (Dar al-Fikr, Beirut), 4th edition, vol. 8, p. 6331 as quoted by Aminurraasyid Yatiban (2003), *The Islamic Concept of Sovereignty: Islamicjerusalem during the First Islamic Conquest as a Case Study.*
25 Baha' al-Din Ibn Shaddad, *Al-Nawadir al-Sultaniyya wa al-Mahsin al-Yusufiyya*, III, p. 265; see also Donald P. Little 'Jerusalem under the Ayyubids and Mamluks', p. 179.
26 This section is based on HH Shaikh Hamdan Bin Rashid Al-Maktoum's Vision for Multiculturalism which was published in 2005 by Al-Maktoum Institute for Arabic and Islamic Studies; and the keynote address 'Al-Maktoum Institute: Practical models for global cross-cultural understanding and cooperation' was delivered by the author in the 34th Scottish Council International Forum *The World We're In* at St Andrew's Bay Hotel and Conference Centre on 18 March 2005. See also the newly published book by Abd al-Fattah El-Awaisi (2007) Setting the new agenda – a unique development of innovation in cultural engagement at academic and communities levels - seven years of excellence: 2000 – 2007 (Al-Maktoum Institute Academic Press)

7

UNDERSTANDING HISTORICAL ISSUES RELATED TO ISLAMICJERUSALEM

In a small booklet published in Arabic in 1991 entitled *The Muslim' scientific, intellectual and cultural presence*, the author presented his argument concerning his methodological approach to understanding history[1]. The aim of this chapter is to present this understanding once more. In addition, it will discuss the claims of some Orientalists and Israeli academics on issues related to Islamicjerusalem.

Historical Methodology

Recording and presenting the human experiences and interpretations of events and their surrounding circumstances in a particular age as it does, history is our knowledge of the past. However, it is also our knowledge of the present and the future because it contains human experiences, both good and evil, that provide humanity with lessons, patterns and models from which to learn. Apart from constituting the nature and the roots of a people or a nation, it is also a depository of people's living experiences, the foundation stones of their buildings and structure, the secret of their strength, the basis of their interaction with the past, and their conscious memory through which the past can be understood, the present can be explained, and the future anticipated. History should not be viewed as merely a category of events compiled only for entertainment nor is it the historian's job to be involved in merely recording past events.

The duty of the historian is to explore the experiences of the past to try to understand the present moment and to plan for the future. An Egyptian scholar and an authority on historical methodology, Hassn Uthman, argues that the knowledge of the past gives humanity "the experience of many years" and enables them to be 'more able to understand themselves and to behave better in the present and future.'[2] A human being's behaviour is governed by his/her experience of the past and his/her expectations for the future. The Algerian thinker, Malik Ibn Nabiy, argues that:

> Our view of history does not only lead to theoretical results but practical ones too that relate to our behaviour in life. They determine our stands towards events and the problems that arise from them[3].

Indeed, history is a chain of interlocking links that make up the course of human civilisations and cultures. History for a human being is the past that lives on into the present and extends into the future. Thus our past is their present (the present of the past generations), and our present is their past (the past of future generations), and our future is their present (the present of future generations). As all ages are governed by the same rules, a person cannot understand his/her being and his/her present and plan for his/her future without understanding his/her past. The human being is the pivotal point around which past, present and future events revolve. A human being is human in the present, past and future. The differences between these three are the differences in the degree of the changing circumstances, environments, places, and times through which those humans live.

One can argue that Islam raised a unique historical awareness of this matter. It laid down a new methodology of dealing with history and a new way of viewing history as a signal unit of time. The present of a nation is the result of its historical course and the beginning of its path towards the future. The Qur'an links a human being's present, past and future. Thus, from a Muslim point of view, history has never been independent knowledge, but part of the wider Muslim knowledge, and linked with the core Muslim disciplines and sciences. It was, for example, a branch or discipline allied to the discipline of the *Hadith* tradition and the discipline of the Qur'an. Moreover, *Sirah* Prophetic Biography was a branch of *Hadith* discipline and its methodology. History also remained a branch of the *Sunnah* way of the Prophet and of *Tafsir* Qur'anic exegesis discipline. Indeed, the Qur'anic treatment of historical knowledge, in particular the stories it relates, has prompted *Tafsir* scholars to search for historical data to help them in their interpretation of the text. Al-Tabari, for example, relies on historical background in his book *Jami al-Bayan fi Tafsir al-Qur'an* (A Collection of Evidence for Interpretation of the Qur'an). Historical knowledge, therefore, became a branch of the Muslim core knowledge, closely linked to the Qur'an.

In short, history is an original and inextricable part of the web of nearly all the human disciplines. Thus, in Muslim history, we find the 'historian narrator', the 'interpreter historian', the 'jurist historian', the 'geographer historian', and so on. Branches of human knowledge are inextricably interwoven and no discipline can be studied in isolation. Accordingly, the best way of studying these disciplines and history in particular is through interdisciplinary and multidisciplinary approaches.

The author concluded the argument on his understanding of history by saying that peoples should not regard their history merely as a refuge from their current situation. History is essential for the progress and stability of any people; they should know and seek inspiration from their history. Any distortion of a nation's history in the eyes of its people will lead inevitably to loss of direction and progress. In short, the nation that survives is the one with a conscience and a true appreciation of its history.

Discussion of the Claims of some Orientalists and Israeli Academics

Islamicjerusalem has always been and will continue to be a major concern for Jews, Christians and Muslims. Due to its religious significances and cultural attachments, feeling often runs very high and even aggressive over Islamicjerusalem. One could argue that it is difficult to adopt a neutral approach in the case of a holy region such as Islamicjerusalem, where the competing claims of the adherents of the three world religions and international interests meet and clash. As has been argued, 'It is quite hard for those who have grown up in a culture, strongly influenced by one of them to stand away from their heritage and to take an objective look at the issue. Indeed, a reader of the available literature on Jerusalem might well lead one to believe that it is impossible. Nevertheless, it is worth trying.'[4]

This position has led on many occasions to the adopting of a biased approach in addressing its issues. Indeed, the history of Islamicjerusalem has suffered distortion, falsification and alteration. Most of the region's historical researches, especially those related to the history of Islamicjerusalem before the first Muslim *Fatih*, are limited to biblical and Orientalist studies. Some Orientalists tend to view Islam as static, timeless, and out of date. One of their main points is their rejection or at least underestimation of Muslim sources and accounts. For example, (see chapter four), they underestimate generally the relevance of the Qur'an and Hadith to the thinking of Muslims and particularly the importance of Islamicjerusalem within the Qur'an and Hadith. They may indeed regard allusions to the Qur'an and Hadith as merely a sort of general piety with little direct bearing on the postures and politics of the Muslims vis-à-vis Islamicjerusalem[5].

As examined in chapter four concerning Umar's Assurance, Muslim historians have presented several accounts on the historic visit of Umar to Aelia which marked the conclusion of the operation of the first Muslim *Fatih* of Aelia. A number of Orientalists and western scholars, such as G. Robert Hoyland[6], Albrecht North[7], and Fred McGraw Donner[8], have critically examined these Muslim accounts and accepted their reliability. However, some Israeli academics and Orientalists have not only cast doubt on the Muslim accounts but even deny that the historic visit of Umar took place. For example, they claim that Sayf Ibn Umar al-Asadi al-Tamimi al-Kufi (died 170 AH/786 C.E.) had a strong bias towards his tribe of Bani Tamim. It may be that he tried to give his tribe some prominence in his accounts of the Muslim *Futuhat* in Iraq where they were part of the Muslim forces there but not in *al-Sham*. This may be what prompted Wellhausen to accuse Sayf lbn Umar somewhat hastily of tilting many historical events in favour of his own school of thought and his own theories of history[9].

Shlomo D. Goitein's hasty accusation of Sayf as having little authenticity and 'whose lack of reliability is well known and whose irresponsibility and ignorance about Palestinian matters' are based on the 'reports about the *Fatih* of Ramla, a town founded by the Muslims only seventy years later'[10], is undoubtedly a trumped-up distortion displaying a shameful bias. It would seem to this author that such bias is not based on any rational academic analysis or objective criticism of the historical sources, but rather, at the very least, on religious and political reasons linked to the struggle of the political institution currently ruling in Israel to gain control of Islamicjerusalem and to lend their establishment a historical legitimacy. The attempt made by some Israeli academics and Orientalists to play down the importance of Islamic sources relating to the period of the first Muslim *Fatih* of Islamicjerusalem and, in particular, to undermine the significance of Islamicjerusalem to Islam, seeks to eliminate other viewpoints and to rewrite the Muslim history of Islamicjerusalem from a single biased point of view. One example of such a bias is Goitein's assertion that the Arab *Fatih* is embellished with imaginary myths and legends, and that consequently there remain only a very few authentic accounts of the stages of the Muslim *Fatih* and the early centuries of Islamicjerusalem life under Muslim rule. In other words, he is attempting to cast doubt on the authenticity of these accounts and the whole process of the first Muslim *Fatih*. He claims that these accounts aim to raise the holy status of Islamicjerusalem in the hearts and minds of Muslims so that they will consider the first Muslim *Fatih* as a major event.[11] On the other hand, Moshe Gill cannot justify Goitein's claim. Gill argues, 'We have seen how Goitein, in his attempt to overcome this contradiction, expressed doubt as to the authenticity of the treaty's (assurance) version as transmitted by Sayf Ibn Umar. But there seems to be little justification for this very stringent attitude towards a source that has been preserved for more than a thousand years.'[12]

However, Goitein's claim is not an isolated one; it represents a trend among Israeli academics. Another example from this group is Herbert Busse who alleges that the first Muslim *Fatih* of Aelia narrated in the Muslim accounts is no more than a myth. He also claims that this, dreamed up by Muslim historians, was an initial step to give Islamicjerusalem a religious holiness, the aim being to replace the Christian character with a Muslim one. To justify his allegations, he presents a weak claim. According to him, to determine the name of the real Muslim conqueror, the Muslim narrators confused the names of *Umar* Ibn al-Khattab and *Amr* Ibn al-As mixing them up. Busse alleges that this was due to the similarity of letters in both names.[13]

However, the current struggle to gain control over Islamicjerusalem has led to the development of these claims and debates between academics on both sides of the conflict, with either nationalist or religious backgrounds. John Gee, the author of one of CAABU briefing, argues that 'seeking to establish a widely accepted common ground of historical understanding is not just an academic exercise, for the past is constantly invoked in situations of conflicts to justify present practice and a future objective and of nowhere is that more true than Jerusalem.'[14] A young Palestinian scholar, Othman al-Tel[15], argues that the Israelis are trying to 'prove' that Islamicjerusalem was 'not important to the Muslims and they did not pay attention to it'. For example, Israelis frequently claim that, as 'a sign of their fundamental indifference to the holy city', 'Muslims never bothered' to make Islamicjerusalem the 'capital of their empire or even the administrative capital of Palestine.'[16]

A respected scholar, Karen Armstrong, disagrees very strongly with the Israeli claim and presents four pieces of evidence in support of her counter argument to reject their allegations. She argues that:

It seems that the Umayyad Caliphs did consider the possibility of making [Islamic] Jerusalem their capital of Damascus. It is ironic that one of the first finds to be unearthed by Israeli archaeologists in (the walled city of) Jerusalem after 1967 was the great Umayyad palace and administrative centre (*Dar al-Imara*) adjoining the southern wall of the Haram (al-Aqsa Mosque). But the (Israeli) project was abandoned. Holy cities are seldom capital cities in the [Muslim] Islamic world. There was no thought of making Makkah the capital instead of Madinah in the early days, despite its superior sanctity. But in the case of [Islamic] Jerusalem, it would clearly also have been difficult to make a city in which Muslims formed only a minority the capital of either a country or a province. And the Christian and Jewish majority in [Islamic] Jerusalem was not the result of Muslim indifference to [Islamic] Jerusalem but of Muslim tolerance.[17]

Indeed, the Muslim rules have not only shown great interest in Islamicjerusalem but have paid a lot of attention to its sanctuary. Although they 'did not even think' of making it 'their capital' or 'the administrative centre for Palestine'[18], they granted Islamicjerusalem special administrative and organisational privileges. The author argues that one major reason for not 'even thinking' of making Islamicjerusalem a capital was, as one of the latest academic serious research findings has it[19], because it is not just a mere city but a region which includes several cities, towns, and villages. During Muslim rule, it was not only an important religious and cultural centre, but a political centre for a number of Muslim rulers and their activities, in particular their political engagements. Several Muslim rulers received their *Bay'a* oath of allegiance in Islamicjerusalem and some of them, such as Mu'awiyya Ibn Abi Sufyan, stayed there for a long period. The name of Aelia was engraved on their minted coins. All these privileges occurred without interfering in non-Muslim affairs or bringing about any unnecessary changes which would contradict the Islamicjerusalem vision. The Muslim policy towards Islamicjerusalem was based on a central principle of making it an open region for all people with diverse backgrounds, not a region restricted only to Muslims.

On the other hand, some Palestinians, as in the case of Khalil Athaminah, are trying also 'to prove that Jerusalem was the administrative capital of Palestine.'[20] Al-Tel concludes his argument on this ongoing debate by stating that the two parties "lack objectivity" in their discussion of the issue, 'The argument between them becomes restricted to saying that, if Jerusalem was not a capital then it was not important and vice versa.'

There any many published works, available to the public, on Palestine and Islamicjerusalem written by Arabs or Muslims for 'different reasons and for specific audiences'[21], but very few can be considered as academic writings. This absence of the Arab and Muslim presence from the academic arena has allowed Orientalists and Israeli academics to fill the gap by marketing their academic works in the Arab and Muslim countries in several ways. For more than a decade, the author has been identifying this unbalanced formula and has urged Arab and Muslim intellectuals to discuss this serious issue critically. He has argued that the Orientalists' work which fills the Arab and Muslim academic arena today has become the only frame of reference. This has, therefore, had serious effects on Arab and Muslim thinking, education, and culture. Such a warring situation has put some serious Arab and Muslim scholars on the defensive, leaving the other parties free to draw up phased strategic plans to achieve their goals. Whenever any Arab and Muslim scholar tries to draw attention to an issue raised by the other side, they are forced into yet another defensive position, and so it goes on.[22]

This applies to the study of Islam and Muslims in general and to the study of Islamicjerusalem in particular. Such a serious position means that there is a lack of a balanced academic work on Islamicjerusalem which is not linked to a political agenda. There is a crucial need for a constructive, innovative, and creative academic alternative to address this issue and fill this gap in the available literature, while at the same time not affiliating itself to any political agenda, neither state nor political party politics. It should also adopt the policy of escaping the trap of reacting to others and trying to engage with them through creating a new agenda, dialogue and debate on the subject. The first step taken in this regard was the foundation of the new field of inquiry of Islamicjerusalem Studies.

---

1   Abd al-Fattah El-Awaisi, *Waqi'una al-Ilmi wa al-Fikri wa al-Thaqafi* (Jerusalem, 1991).
2   Hassan Uthman, *The historical methodology* (Cairo, 1943), p. 13.
3   Malik Ibn Nabiy, *Ta'amulat* (Beirut, 1979), p. 126.
4   John Gee, *The question of Jerusalem: historical perspectives*, CAABU briefing, no. 40, November 1995, p. 1.
5   Abd al-Fattah El-Awaisi 'The significance of Jerusalem in Islam: an Islamic reference', p. 48.
6   G. Robert Hoyland, *Seeing Islam as others saw it: a survey and evaluation of Christian, Jewish and Zoroastrian writings on early Islam* (Princeton, 1992), pp. 64-65.
7   Albrecht North, *The early Arabic historical tradition: a source critical study* (translated by M. Bonner), 2nd edition (Princeton, 1994), pp. 181.
8   Fred McGraw Donner, *The early Islamic conquest* (Princeton, 1981), pp. 151-153.
9   Wellhausen, Skizzen und Vorarbeiten Heft IV, cited by Israel Ben Zeev (Abu Zuaib), *Ka'ab al-Ahbar: Jews and Judaism in the Islamic Tradition*, p. 37.
10 Shlomo D. Goitein 'Jerusalem in the Arab period: 638-1099', p. 171. However, Moshe Gil argues that 'there seems to be little justification for this very stringent attitude (of Goitein) towards a source that has been preserved for more than a thousand years'. Moshe Gil, *A History of Palestine: 634-1099*, p. 73.
11 Shlomo D. Goitein, 'Jerusalem in the Arab period: 638-1099', p. 169. See also the same author 'Al-Kuds', Encyclopaedia of Islam (new edition).
12 Moshe Gil, *A History of Palestine: 634-1099*, p. 73.
13 Herbert Busse 'Omar B. al-Hattab in Jerusalem' *Journal of Jerusalem Studies in Arabic and Islam,* 5 (1984), pp. 73-119; and 'Omar's Image as the conqueror of Jerusalem' *Journal of Jerusalem Studies in Arabic and Islam,* 8 (1986), pp. 149-168.
14 John Gee, *The question of Jerusalem: historical perspectives*, p. 1.

15   Othman Ismael Al-Tel, *The first Islamic conquest of Aelia (Islamicjerusalem): A critical analytical study of the early Islamic historical narrations and sources*, p. 266; see also pp. 264-276.

16   Armstrong disagrees very strongly with this claim, as will be discussed later on. Karen Armstrong 'Sacred Space: the Holiness of Islamicjerusalem', pp. 15.

17   Ibid., p. 15.

18   Othman Ismael Al-Tel, *The first Islamic conquest of Aelia (Islamicjerusalem): A critical analytical study of the early Islamic historical narrations and sources*, p. 227.

19   The background of this latest research has been discussed in footnote 2 in chapter two.

20   Khalil Athamina, *Filastin fi Khamsat Qurun, min al-Fatth al-Islami hatta al-Ghazu al-Firaniji: 634-1099*, pp. 205-219.

21   Aisha al-Ahlas, *Islamic Research Academy: 1994-2004, background, activities and achievements, with special reference to the new field of inquiry of Islamicjerusalem Studies*, p. 9.

22   Abd al-Fattah El-Awaisi, *Waqiuna al-Ilmi wa al-Fikri wa al-Thaqafi*, pp. 34-35.

CONCLUSION

Islamicjerusalem is claimed as a sacred space by three of the world's major monotheistic religions: Judaism, Christianity, and Islam. Although Islamicjerusalem is the most delicate issue of dispute between the current two conflicting parties, it is hoped that this book will provide a better understanding for the world leaders who are trying to return peace to the region. When the author thinks of Islamicjerusalem, he thinks of several concepts including those of hope and justice. One could argue that 'history has proved that there can never be peace nor stability without justice. The road to peace starts in Islamicjerusalem and the solution of its current issue is the key to a just peace in the region.'[1] As Karen Armstrong argue in her paper at the 1997 International Academic Conference on Islamicjerusalem:

> From the very earliest days, it seems the cult of Jerusalem was inextricably bound up with the quest for social justice. Thus in the Hebrew Bible, prophets and psalmists repeatedly reminded their people that Jerusalem could not be a holy city of *Shalom* (of peace) unless it was also a city of *Tseddeq* (of justice)[2].

Michael Prior adds that:

> The lesson of history is that it cannot belong exclusively to one people or to only one religion. Jerusalem should be open to all, shared by all. Those who govern the city should make it 'the capital of humankind'[3].

The first Muslim *Fatih* of Islamicjerusalem, five years after the death of Prophet Muhammad (12 Rabi' al-Awal 11 AH/ 6 **June**

632 CE), was a natural progression. The initial practical steps taken
by Prophet Muhammad helped to create a supportive environment
and to establish and direct future events. Indeed, they were
preliminary steps on the way to the great campaign which was
launched and directed by the first Caliph, Abu Bakr, at *al-Sham* and
crowned by the conquering of Islamicjerusalem by the second
Caliph, Umar Ibn al-Khattab in Jumada I/II 16 AH/ **June**/July
637 CE. Indeed, if Prophet Muhammad's Night Journey was a
turning point for both Muslims and Islamicjerusalem, the first
Muslim *Fatih* of Islamicjerusalem was a radical turning point in
history in general and in Muslim Arab history in particular.

The Muslims' devotion to Islamicjerusalem is not a result of
colonialist aims or a desire to expand their rule, nor is it based on
false racist nationalist claims. On the contrary, the nature of
Islamicjerusalem and its special qualities constitute the
fundamental reason for their concern for it. In the seventh
century, and in particular during the first Muslim *Fatih* of
Islamicjerusalem, the land of hope provided the world with the
famous document known as Umar's Assurance of Safety *Aman* to
the people of Aelia (Islamicjerusalem). This fundamental landmark
of hope laid the foundations for future relations and led to
reshaping the relationships between people of diverse faiths who
inhabited the region, namely, Jews, Christians and Muslims. This
marked the beginning of a new and distinguished era of safety,
peace, stability, security, progress, development and prosperity.

With a global feeling and a local touch, Umar was trying to resolve
a local conflict with an international approach. In other words, he
was 'thinking globally' and 'acting locally'. Indeed, Umar's
Assurance was the jewel of the first Muslim *Fatih* of Aelia, and the
beacon for developing Islamicjerusalem's unique and creative
vision and nature.

Umar's Assurance of Safety not only rejected the notion of the
supremacy of one people or race over others but presented
Islamicjerusalem as a model both for multiculturalism and for
conflict resolution. As one of the main characteristics of

Islamicjerusalem is its competing political and religious claims, one could argue that it should be presented as a model for conflict resolution through constructive argumentation methodology as a means for a 'constructive dialogue' and positive negotiation with its conflicting parties. The adopting of this constructive dialogue methodology would open the way for conflict resolution.

At the beginning of the twenty-first century, and in particular through serious scholarly findings, the land of hope is representing itself in a modern fashion as a model for multiculturalism. Indeed, our understanding of Islamicjerusalem as a model for multiculturalism with all its intertwined elements, nature, characteristics, as presented in this book, could be seen as the twenty-first century's contribution to establishing a new agenda and new frame of reference for safety, peace, stability, security, progress, development and prosperity in the region. In short, Umar's global vision and local focus presented Islamicjerusalem as a model for multiculturalism.

In conclusion, the question which needs to be asked here is: what are the relationships between *Barakah, Amal*, and *Aman*? Between the land of *Barakhah*, the land *Amal* (hope), and the product of the vision of this land? Umar Assurance of *Aman* (Safety). The author argues that hope is one of the manifestations of the *Barakah*; and hope travels with the *Barakhah*. This means that Islamicjerusalem is the centre of both *Barakah* and hope. The land of hope is open and inclusive to everyone without any discrimination. It should be an open land to anyone wishing to seek refuge and serenity. What is most interesting here is the link between all these terminologies, which demonstrates Islamicjerusalem's centrality and universal character. They are supported by referring to the core Muslim sources but with new interpretations of these.

Indeed, the establishment of this link with Islamicjerusalem has acted as a major factor in bringing Arab and Muslim unity and is a true measure of Arab and Muslim power or weakness. It has acted also as a mirror, reflecting the situation of the Muslims in general and the Arabs in particular. The author argues that the status of

Islamicjerusalem is linked with the status of Arabs and Muslims, and the future of Islamicjerusalem is linked with their future. For example, whenever Islamicjerusalem has been liberated and ruled by Arab-Muslims, this indicates that they are at the peak of their power. However, when they lose power and fall into decay, they lose Islamicjerusalem. Indeed, the Arabs and Muslims have no real power or impact without Islamicjerusalem.

On the other hand, contemporary Muslim Jerusalem is shaped in part by dialogue with the concept of Islamicjerusalem, the classical and modern history of Muslims, and in part by response to external interests and influences in the region. Accordingly, contemporary Muslims seek to relate their heritage in Muslim Jerusalem from the concept of Islamicjerusalem and Muslim past to the radical situation of today.

The unique aspect of Islamicjerusalem is highlighted through its vision, which presents a model for peaceful co-existence and mutual respect. It also offers a way for people from different religious and cultural backgrounds to live together in an environment of multiculturalism, and religious and cultural engagement, diversity and tolerance.

In short, Islamicjerusalem is not a mere city nor yet another urban settlement, but a region which includes several cities, towns, and villages of which al-Aqsa Mosque is the centre. It gives the world a model of a common space in which people from different backgrounds can live together in peaceful co-existence and mutual respect. It is described in the Qur'an as a place 'surrounded with *Barakah*'; which means that it radiates *Barakah*. Indeed, it is not closed and insular, but a centre in which diversity and pluralism thrive through mutual respect and co-existence. Indeed, identifying the centre of the *Barakah* led the author to develop a new significant innovative theory, *the Barakah Circle Theory of Islamicjerusalem.*

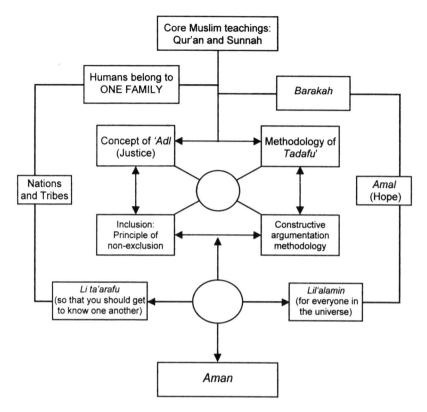

Diagram 6: Islamicjerusalem models for peaceful
co-existence and mutual respect

Several supporting pieces of evidence have been provided to support the author's central argument that **Islamicjerusalem** is not exclusive but **inclusive** and should be opened up 'to everyone in the universe', as stated in the Qur'an *Lil'alamin* (Qur'an, 21:71), 'so that you should get **to know** one another' *Li ta'arafu* (Qur'an, 49:13), not that you may despise one another. This unique global common space of openness and *Barakah* has made Islamicjerusalem an ideal *Amal* region where the one human family can make *Li ta'arafu*, live together in *Aman* and enjoy this *Barakah*.

1   Abd al-Fattah El-Awaisi, 'The significance of Jerusalem in Islam: an Islamic reference', p. 47.

2   Karen Armstrong, 'Sacred Space: the Holiness of Islamicjerusalem', p. 7.

3   Michael Prior, 'Christian perspectives on Jerusalem', p. 17.

BIBLIOGRAPHY

Translation of the Meaning of the Qur'an

Abdel Haleem, M.A.S. (2004), *The Qur'an: a new translation* (Oxford University Press).

Ali, Abdullah Yusuf (2003), *The Meaning of the Holy Qur'an* (Islamic Foundation, Leicester).

Asad, Muhammad (2003),*The Message of the Qur'an* (Book Foundation, England).

Cleary, Thomas (2004), The Qur'an: a new translation (Starlatch Press, USA).

Khan, Muhammad Muhsin and Al-Hilali, Muhammad Taqi-ud-Din (1996), *Interpretation of the Meaning of the Noble Qur'an* (Dar-us-Salam, Saudi Arabia).

Primary Sources

Al-Andalusiy, Abd Allah al-Bakiri (1947), *Mu'jam ma Istu'jim* (Cairo).

Al-Azdi, Muhammad Ibn Abd Allah (1970), *Tarikh Futuh al-Sham* (ed. by A. Amer, Mu'assasat Sijil al-Arab, Cairo).

Al-Baladhuri, Muhammad (1936), *Futuh al-Buldan* (Cairo).

Al-Bukhari (n.d.), *Sahih al-Bukhari bi Hashiat al-Sanadi* (Dar al-Ma'rifiah, Beirut).

Al-Ghayti, Najm al-Din Muhammad Ibn Ahmad (1986), *Al-Jawab al-Qawim an al-Su'al al-Mut'alliq bi Iqta' al-Sayyid Tamim* (edited by Hassan Abd al-Rahman al-Silwadi), (Islamic Research Centre, Jerusalem).

Ibn Asakir (1329-1332AH), *Tarikh Madinat Dimashq* (Damascus).

Ibn al-Athir (1982), *Al-Kamil fi al-Tarikh* (Beirut).

Ibn al-Batriq (Eutychius), Said (1905), *Al-Tarikh al-Majmu'* (Beirut).

Ibn al-Jawzi (1979), *Fada 'il al-Quds* (Beirut).

Ibn al-Jawzi, Abu al-Faraj Abd al-Rahman Ibn Ali (ed. 2001), *Sirat wa Manaqb Amir al-Mu'minin Umar Ibn al-Khattab* (ed. by M. Amr, Dar al-Da'wah al-Islamiyyah, Cairo).

Ibn Hisham (1987), *Al-Sira Al-Nabawiyya* (Dar Al-Rayan lil-Turath, Cairo).

Ibn Kathir (1978), *AI-Bidayah wa al-Nihayyah* (Beirut).

Ibn Kathir (n.d.), *Al-Sira Al-Nabawiyya* (Dar Ihya' Al-Turath Al'Arabi, Beirut).

Ibn Sa'd, Muhammad (1985), *Al-Tabaqat al-Kubra* (Beirut).

Ibn Sallam, Abu Ubayed al-Qasim (1986), *Kitab Al-Amwal* (Beirut).

Ibn Shaddad, Baha' al-Din (1964), *AI-Nawadir al-Sultaniyya wa al-Mahsin al-Yusufiyya* (Cairo).

Al-Jawziyyah, Ibn al-Qayyim (n.d.), *Al-Turuq al-Hukmiyyah fi al-Siyasah al-Shar'iyyah* (edited by Muhammad Jamil Ghazi, Matba'at al-Madaina).

Al-Maqdisi, Abu Abd Allah Muhammad (1909), *Ahsan al-Taqasim Fi Ma'rift al-Aqalim* (Brill, Leiden), 2nd edition.

Al-Maqdisi, Muhammad (1977), *Ahsan al-Taqasim fi Ma'rifat al-Aqalim* (Baghdad).

Muslim (1978), *Sahih Muslim wa al-Jami' al-Sahih* (Beirut), 2nd edition.

Al-Muti'i, Shaikh Muhammad Bakhit (1984), *Copy of the Ruling by His Eminence Shaikh Muhammad Bakhit Al-Muti'i, former Mufti of Egypt, on the Waqf of the Prophet's Companion Tamim Al-Dari and his successors*, issued on 7 Rajab 1350 AH, No. 275, p. 99, Part 7 (Islamic Vocational Orphanage, Jerusalem)

Al-Tabari (1960), *Tarikh al-Rusul wa al-Muluk* (Cairo).

Al-Tabari (1988), *Tarikh al-Rusul wa al-Muluk* (Beirut), 2nd edition.

Al-'Ulaimi, Mujir al-Din (1977), *AI-Uns al-Jalil bi tarikh al-Quds wa al-Khalil* (Amman).

Al-'Ulaimi Al-Hanbali, Mujir al-Din (1973) *Al-Uns al-Jalil bi Tarikh al-Quds wa al-Khalil* (Al-Muhtassib Bookshop, Amman).

Al-Waqidi, Muhammad Ibn Umar (1954), *Futuh al-Sham* (Cairo).

Al-Waqidi, Muhammad Ibn Umar (n.d.), *Futuh al-Sham* (Al-Muhtassib Bookshop, Amman).

Al-Waqidi M. (n.d.), *Futuh al-Sham* (edited by H. al-Hajj, al-Maktaba al-Tawfiqiyah, Cairo).

William of Tyre, (trans. 1976), *A history of deeds done beyond the sea*, translated and annotated by E.A. Babcock Octagon Books (New York).

AI-Ya'qubi (1960), *Tarikh al-Ya'qubi* (Beirut).

Unpublished Research and Documents

Abd Rahman, Fatimatuzzahra' (2004), Political, Social and Religious Changes in Islamicjerusalem from the First Islamic *Fatih* until the end of Umayyad period (637 to 750CE): An Analytical Study (Unpublished Master's dissertation, Al-Maktoum Institute for Arabic and Islamic Studies).

Abu-Munshar, Maher Younes (2003), A Historical Study of Muslim Treatment of Christians in Islamicjerusalem at the Time of Umar Ibn al-Khattab and Salah al-Din with Special Reference to the Islamic Values of Justice (Unpublished PhD thesis, Al-Maktoum Institute for Arabic and Islamic Studies).

El-Awaisi, Abd al-Fattah (2005), 'Al-Maktoum Institute: Practical models for global cross-cultural understanding and co-operation' a keynote address in the 34th Scottish Council International Forum *The World We're In* at St Andrew's Bay Hotel and Conference Centre on 18 March 2005.

El-Awaisi, Abd al-Fattah (2007), *Setting the New Agenda – A Unique Development of Innovation in Cultural Engagement at Academic and Communities Levels - Seven Years of Excellence: 2000 – 2007* (Al-Maktoum Institute Academic Press).

El-Awaisi, Khalid Abd al-Fattah (2003), *Geographical Boundaries of Islamicjerusalem"* (Unpublished Master's dissertation, Al-Maktoum Institute for Arabic and Islamic Studies).

Hassan, Sarah Mohamed Sherif Abdel-Aziz (2005), *Women: Active Agents in Islamising Islamicjerusalem from the Prophet's Time until the End of the Umayyed Period*" (Unpublished Master's dissertation, Al-Maktoum Institute for Arabic and Islamic Studies).

Ibrahim, Ramona Ahmed (2005) *Islamicjerusalem as a model of conflict resolution: a case study of the negotiations between Salah al-Din and Richard the Lionheart (1191 – 1192 CE).* (Unpublished Master's dissertation, Al-Maktoum Institute for Arabic and Islamic Studies).

Jabaren, Ra'ed (2006) *Muslim juristic rulings of Islamicjerusalem with special reference to Ibadat in Al-Aqsa Mosque: A critical comparative study.* (Unpublished PhD thesis, Al-Maktoum Institute for Arabic and Islamic Studies).

Kazmouz, Mahmoud Mataz (2006) *The Ottoman implementation of the vision of Islamicjerusalem as a model for multiculturalism with a special reference to Sultan Suleiman I, the magnificent (1520 – 1566).* (Unpublished Master's dissertation, Al-Maktoum Institute for Arabic and Islamic Studies).

Al-Maktoum, Hamdan Bin Rashid (2005), *HH Shaikh Hamdan Bin Rashid Al-Maktoum's Vision for Multiculturalism* (Al-Maktoum Institute for Arabic and Islamic Studies).

Mohammad Nor, Mohammad Roslan (2005) *The significance of Islamicjerusalem in Islam: Qur'anic and Hadith perspectives.*

Omar, Abdallah Ma'rouf (2005) *Towards the conquest of Islamicjerusalem: the three main practical steps taken by Prophet Muhammad – Analytical study.* (Unpublished Master's dissertation, Al-Maktoum Institute for Arabic and Islamic Studies).

Yatiban, Aminurraasyid (2003), *The Islamic Concept of Sovereignty: Islamicjerusalem during the First Islamic Conquest as a Case Study* (Unpublished Master's dissertation, Al-Maktoum Institute for Arabic and Islamic Studies).

Yatiban, Aminurraasyid (2006), *Muslim understandings of the concept of Al-Siyada (sovereignty): an analytical study of Islamicjerusalem from the first*

Muslim conquest until the end of the first Abasid period (16-264AH/637-877CE) (Unpublished PhD thesis, Al-Maktoum Institute for Arabic and Islamic Studies).

Articles in Journals

Ajin, Ali (1417 AH), 'Al-Uhda al-Umariyya', *Al-Hikma Journal* (no. 10).

Armstrong, Karen (1997), 'Sacred Space: the Holiness of Islamicjerusalem', *Journal of Islamicjerusalem Studies* (vol. I, no. I, Winter 1997).

El-Awaisi, Abd al-Fattah (1998), 'The significance of Jerusalem in Islam: an Islamic reference' *Journal of Islamicjerusalem Studies*, vol. 1, no. 2 (Summer 1998).

El-Awaisi, Abd al-Fattah (2000), 'Umar's Assurance of Safety to the People of Aelia (Jerusalem): A Critical Analytical Study of the Historical Sources' *Journal of Islamicjerusalem Studies* vol. 3, no. 2 (Summer 2000), pp. 47-89.

Busse, Herbert (1984), 'Omar B. al-Hattab in Jerusalem' *Journal of Jerusalem Studies in Arabic and Islam*, 5 (1984).

Busse, Herbert (1986), 'Omar's Image as the conqueror of Jerusalem' *Journal of Jerusalem Studies in Arabic and Islam*, 8 (1986).

Al-Buti, Muhammad Said (1999), 'Mu'amalit al-Dawlah al-Islamiyyah li ghaiyr al-Muslimin: al-Quds Namwudhajan', *Journal of Islamicjerusalem Studies* (no. 1, vol. 3, Winter 1999).

Drory, Joseph (1981), 'Jerusalem during the Mamluk period: 1250-1517', *The Jerusalem Cathedra*.

Goitein, Shlomo D. (1982), 'Jerusalem in the Arab period: 638-1099', *The Jerusalem Cathedra*, 2.

Little, Donald (1985), 'Haram Documents related to the Jews of late fourteenth century Jerusalem', *Journal of Semitic Studies* (vol. 30, no. 2, 1985).

Prior, Michael (1999), 'Christian perspectives on Jerusalem', *Journal of Islamicjerusalem Studies*, vol. 3, no.1 (Winter 1999).

Al-Qaradawi, Yusuf (1997), 'Al-Quds fi al-Wa'yi al-Islami', *Journal of Islamicjerusalem Studies* (no. 1, vol. 1, Winter 1997).

Al-Ratrout, Haithem (2005), 'Al-Masjid al-Aqsa fi al-Athar al-Qur'aniah' *Journal of Islamicjerusalem Studies*, vol. 6, no.1 (Summer 2005).

Al-Sharif, Abd Allah (1424 AH), 'Mawqif Yahud al-Sham min *al-Fatih al-Islami*', *Majalat Jami'at Umm al-qura li Ulum al-Shari'a wa al-Lugha al-Arabia wa Adabiha* vol. 16, No. 28 (Shawwal 1424 AH).

Secondary Sources

Abdul-Raof, Hussein (2003), *Exploring the Qur'an* (Al-Maktoum Institute Academic Press, Scotland).

Al-Ahlas, Aisha (2004), *Islamic Research Academy: 1994-2004, background, activities and achievements, with special reference to the new field of inquiry of Islamicjerusalem Studies* (ISRA, Scotland).

Abu-Munshar, Maher (2007), *Islamic Jerusalem and Its Christians: A History of Tolerance and Tensions* (I B Tauris & Co Ltd).

Abu al-Rub, Hani (2002), *Tarikh Filastin fi Sadr al-Islam* (Jerusalem).

Armstrong, Karen (1996), *A History of Jerusalem: One City. Three Faiths* (HarperCollins Publishers, London).

Al-Arif, Arif (1961), *Al-Mufassal fi Tarikh al-Quds* (al-Andalus Library, Jerusalem).

Asali, K.J. (1989), 'Jerusalem under the Ottomans: 1516-1831 AD' in K.J. Asali (ed.), *Jerusalem in History* (Scorpion Publishing, Essex).

Athamina, Khalil (2000), *Filastin fi Khamsat Qurun, min al-Fatih al-Islami hatta al-Ghazu al-Firaniji: 634-1099* (The Institute for Palestine Studies, Beirut).

Atwan, Hussain (1986), *al-Riwaiyat al-Tarikhia fi Bilad al-Sham fi al-Asr al-Amawi* (Amman).

El-Awaisi, Abd al-Fattah (1989), *Darih wa Masjid al-Sahabi al-Jalil Tamim Ibn Aws Al-Dari, Radiya Allahu 'anhu: 1917-1948* (Jerusalem).

El-Awaisi, Abd al-Fattah (1991), *Waqi'una al-Ilmi wa al-Fikri wa al-Thaqafi* (Jerusalem).

El-Awaisi, Abd al-Fattah (1997), *Makanit wa Tarikh Bayt al-Maqdis* (Islamic Research Academy, Scotland).

El-Awaisi, Khalid (2007), *Mapping Islamicjerusalem: a Rediscovery of Geographical Boundaries* (Al-Maktoum Institute Academic Press).

Al-Azawi, Abd al-Rahman (1989), *Al-Tabari* (Baghdad).

Al-Basit, Musa Isma'il (2001), *al-Uhda al-Umariyya bayn al-Qubul wa al-Rad: Dirasah Naqdiyyah* (Jerusalem).

Ben Zeev (Abu Zuaib), Israel (1976), *Ka'ab al-Ahbar: Jews and Judaism in the Islamic Tradition* (Jerusalem).

Cohen, Amnon (1984), *Jewish life under Islam: Jerusalem in the sixteenth century* (Harvard University Press).

Crone, Patricia and Cook, Michael (1977), *Hagarism: the Making of the Islamic World* (Cambridge University Press).

Donner, Fred McGraw (1981), *The Early Islamic Conquests* (Princeton University Press, New Jersey).

Duri, Abdul Aziz (1989), 'Jerusalem in the Early Islamic period: 7th-11th centuries AD' in K.J. Asali (ed.), *Jerusalem in History* (Scorpion Publishing, Essex).

Foss, Michael (2002), *People of the first Crusades* (Caxton, London).

Gee, John (1995), *The question of Jerusalem: historical perspectives* (CAABU briefing, no. 40).

Goitein, Shlomo D., 'Al-Kuds', *Encyclopaedia of Islam* (new edition).

Gil, Moshe (1992), *A History of Palestine: 634-1099* (Cambridge University Press).

Hitti, Philip (1957), *Tarikh al-Arab* (Beirut).

Hiyari, Mustafa A. (1989), 'Crusader Jerusalem: 1099 - 1187 AD' in K.J. Asali (ed.), *Jerusalem in History* (Scorpion Publishing, Essex).

Hoyland, G. Robert (1992), *Seeing Islam as others saw it: a survey and evaluation of Christian, Jewish and Zoroastrian writings on early Islam* (Princeton).

Ibn Nabiy, Malik (1979), *Ta'amulat* (Beirut).

Ibshirly, Muhammad and Al-Tamimi, Muhammad Dawud (1982), *Awqaf wa Amlak Al-Muslimin fi Filistin* (Centre for Researches in Islamic History, Arts and Culture, Istanbul).

Jasir, Shafiq (1989), *Tarikh al-Quds* (Amman).

Jasir, Shafiq (1999), 'Al-Taghayyurat al-Diymughrafiyah fi al-Quds Abra Tarikhuha' in Shafiq Jasir (ed.), *Jerusalem fi al-Khitab al-Mu'asir* (Jordan).

Lane-Poole, Stanley (1985), *Saladin and the fall of the Kingdom of Jerusalem* (Dare Publishers, London).

Little, Donald P. (1989), 'Jerusalem under the Ayyubids and Mamluks' in K. J. Asali (ed.), *Jerusalem in History* (Scorpion Publishing, Essex).

Al-Nadawi, Abu al-Hassan (1981), *Al-Sira al-Nabawiyya* (Al-Maktaba al-Asriya, Sidon).

North, Albrecht (1994), *The early Arabic historical tradition: a source critical study* (translated by M. Bonner), 2nd edition (Princeton, 1994).

Prawer, J. (1964), 'Minorities in the Crusader states' in *A History of the Crusades* (New York).

Al-Quda, Zakariyya (1987), 'Mu'ahadit *Fatih* Bayt al-Maqdis: al-Uhda al-Umariyya' in Muhammad Adnan al-Bakhit and Ihsan Abass (eds), *Bilad al-Sham fi Sadir al-Islam* (University of Jordan and University of Yarmuk, Jordan), vol. 2.

Ranciman, Steven (1965), *A History of the Crusades* (London).

Ranciman, Steven (1987), *A History of the Crusades* (Cambridge Academic Press, Cambridge).

Al-Ratrout, Haitham (2004), *The architectural development of al-Aqsa Mosque in the early Islamic period: Sacred architecture in the shape of the 'Holy'* (Al-Maktoum Institute Academic Press).

Rustum, Asad (1939), *Mustalah al-Tarikh* (Beirut).

Sahas, Daniel J. (1994), 'Patriarch Sophronious, Umar Ibn al-Khattab and the *Fatih* of Jerusalem', in Hadia Dajani-Shakeel and Burhan Dajani, *Al-Sira' al-Islami al-Faranji ala Filastin fi al-Qurun al-Wasta (The Islamic - Frankish (Ifranj) conflict over Palestine during the Middle Ages* (The Institute for Palestine Studies, Beirut).

Sakhnini, Issam (2001), *Ahd Ilya wa al-Shurut al-Umariyya* (Amman).

Scott, Joan Wallach (1999), *Gender and the Politics of History* (Columbia University Press, New York).

Al-Sharif, Ahmad (1976), *Dirast fl al-Hadarah al-Islamiyyah* (Cairo).

Al-Tel, Othman Ismael (2003), *The first Islamic conquest of Aelia (Islamicjerusalem): A critical analytical study of the early Islamic historical narrations and sources* (Al-Maktoum Institute Academic Press, Scotland).

Tritton, A.S. (1930), *The Caliphs and their non-Muslim Subjects* (Oxford).

Uthman, Hassan (1943), *The historical methodology* (Cairo).

Wilkinson, John (1989), 'Jerusalem under Rome and Byzantium: 63 BC - 637 AD' in K.J. Asali (ed.), *Jerusalem in History* (Scorpion Publishing, Essex).

Al-Zuhayli, Wahbah (2002), Al-Fiqh al-Islami wa Adillatuh (Dar al-Fikr, Beirut), 4th edition.

INDEX

A

Abd Allah Ibn Nusaibah, 115
Abd al-Rahman Ibn Awf, 58, 63, 77
Abdullah Ibn Salih, 68
Abu Bakr, 25, 46, 47, 48, 49, 103, 142
Abu Dhar, 32, 33
Abu Hafs al-Dimashqi, 58, 60
Abu Talib, 38
Abu Ubayda, 75, 118
Abu Ubayed, 68
'Adl (Justice), 5, 86, 96-97, 100, 105, 111, 119
Aelia, 5, 9, 11-12, 17, 25, 44, 55-60, 62-75, 80, 83-86, 89-91, 102, 111, 114, 117, 134, 136-137, 142
Aelia region, 11, 66, 75
Ahadith, 15-16
Ahl al-Ard, 62, 65-67
Ahmad Ibn Hanbal, 39
Ali Ibn Abi Talib, 61
Al-ladhi Barakna Hawlahu, 23, 27
Alqamah Ibn Mujzz, 46
Amr Ibn Al-Aas, 25
Al-Aqsa Mosque, 7, 10-11, 17, 18, 23, 27, 28, 31-33, 35, 37, 39, 69, 73-74, 78, 137, 144
Arab, 3, 9, 49, 57, 61, 68, 70, 75, 78, 79, 82, 117, 119, 125, 127, 135, 138, 142, 143
Arabian Peninsula, 30, 41, 48

Al-Ardh al-Mubaraka, 30
Al-Arisiyyin, 44
Armenians, 77, 80
Awf Ibn Malik, 42
Ayla (Aqabah), 46

B

Al-Baladhuri, 58, 60, 68, 75, 82
Barakah, 5, 10, 23, 24, 27, 28, 30, 37, 40, 41, 116, 143-145
Barakah Circle Theory, 2, 5, 10, 23, 28, 41, 144
Bay'a (oath), 137
Bayt al-Maqdis, 11, 13, 20, 57, 59, 70, 74, 80, 90
Beersheba, 27
Bethlehem, 77
Birr (love and compassion), 98
Boundaries of Islamicjerusalem, 5, 18, 24-26, 45
British Mandate, 43, 82
Byzantines, 44-45, 48, 51, 62-63, 65-66, 70-71, 110, 117, 118

C

Cairo Geniza, 72, 91
Canaanites, 39
Christian Jerusalem, 12

Christians, 17, 24, 57, 70, 72-73, 75, 77, 80, 82, 84, 85, 110, 115-118, 133, 142
Constructive argumentation, 99
Copts, 77, 80
Crusades, 64, 69, 73, 121

D

Dawmat al-Jandal, 45-46
Dhimmi, 75-76

E

East Syrians, 80
Egypt, 30, 48, 50, 68, 72, 100, 111, 119
Eutychius, 57, 58, 59, 82, 114

G

Gaza, 27, 50
Al-Ghazali, 43, 51

H

Hadith, 16, 18, 32, 62, 133, 134
Hadrian, 72, 80, 84, 89, 117
Al-Haram Mosque, 27, 31, 32, 37
Haroun al-Rashid, 83, 93
Hawlahu (surrounded), 27
Hebron, 27, 43
Heraclius, 44, 51, 70, 80, 89
Hijaz, 60
Hijra, 38, 41, 76-79
Holy House, 11
Holy Sepulchre, 77, 81, 91, 114-115

I

Ibn al-Ibri, 117
Ibn al-Qayyim al-Jawziyya, 56
Ibn Asakir, 83
Ilahiyyat, 16
Islamic Quds, 12
Islamicjerusalem Studies, 1-5, 7-15, 17, 19, 20, 35, 50, 89, 104, 122, 139
Israel, 135
Istanbul, 27, 33, 76, 82

J

Jacobites, 77, 80
Jaffa, 27
Jerusalem, 7, 9, 11-12, 19, 27, 43, 51, 57, 68-69, 72-73, 76, 78, 80, 82, 84, 85, 89, 91, 93, 94, 102, 104, 110, 116, 134, 136-138, 141
Jewish Jerusalem, 12
Jews, 24, 56, 58-60, 62, 69, 70-75, 78, 84-85, 89-90, 92, 94, 98-99, 101, 110, 116-119, 133, 142
Jizya tax, 44, 59, 62, 64-65, 68, 74, 77, 83, 85, 117

K

Ka'bah, 23, 32, 33, 41
Khadijah, 38
Khalid Ibn al-Walid, 46, 58, 63
Khalid Ibn Sa'id, 48
Kharaj tax, 75
King Richard I, 102, 103, 122
Kufa, 60

L

Land of Amal (hope), 5, 37, 39, 40, 42, 116, 142, 143
Land of Barakah, 23
Li ta'arafu, 109, 145
Lil'alamin, 39, 40, 145

M

Madinah, 24, 41-43, 45-47, 52, 58, 61, 99-101, 116, 137
Makkah, 23-24, 27, 30-33, 37-42, 45, 116, 137
Mamluk period, 74
Maronites, 77, 80
Al-Mi'raj, 38
Monophysite Christians, 118
Mount of Olives, 73, 76, 78
Mount Zion, 72
Mu'tah, 45, 52
Mu'awiyah Ibn Abi Sufyan, 58, 63
Mujir al-Din al-'Ulaimi, 68, 83
Multiculturalism, 13, 109, 122, 129
Muslim Jerusalem, 12, 144

N

Nablus, 50, 75
Al-Nawawi, 102
Nebuchadnezzar, 71
Nestorian, 77, 80, 118
Night Journey, 23, 32, 34, 37-42, 49, 50, 103, 142

O

Walled city of Jerusalem, 7, 11, 137
Orientalist studies, 134
Orthodox Patriarchate in Jerusalem, 5, 56, 76, 84
Othman Ibn Afan, 77
Ottoman period, 27, 35, 79, 81
Ownership (Milkiya), 120

P

Palestine, 7, 25, 43, 50-51, 74-75, 90-91, 99, 136-138
Patriarch Sophronius, 70, 72, 81, 84
Principle of non-exclusion, 98
Prophet Abraham, 24, 32, 39, 116
Prophet Joshua, 48
Prophet Muhammad, 4, 11, 18, 23, 31-32, 34, 37-49, 52-53, 76, 80, 97, 101, 109, 116, 141
Prophet Solomon, 71

Q

Al-Quds al-Islamiyyah, 12

R

Al-Ramla Peace Treaty, 103
Romans, 44, 71, 117

S

Sa'id Ibn al-Batriq, 114
Safiyyah Bint Huyayyi Ibn Akhtab, 16
Al-Sahifah(The Constitution of Madinah), 101

Salah al-Din, 17, 19, 30, 74, 92, 94, 102-104, 118, 121
Sayf Ibn Umar, 60-61, 82-84, 134, 136
Shaddad Ibn Aws, 42
Al-Sham (Syria), 30, 42, 45, 47, 48-49, 75, 135, 142
Al-Shurut al-Umariyya, 56
Sinai, 30, 48, 72
Sulh (peace), 46, 75
Sunnah, 96, 98, 111, 114, 133

T

Al-Tabari, 5, 51, 56-64, 67, 69-70, 82-84, 133
Tabuk, 42, 45, 52
Tadafu' (counteraction), 5, 96, 100, 105, 111
Tafsir, 24, 133
Tamim Ibn Aws Al-Dari, 43
Titus, 72

U

Al-Uhda al-Umariyya. See Umar's Assurance of Safety
Umar Ibn al-Khattab, 12, 17, 47-49, 55-59, 61, 66-67, 70-72, 74, 76, 79-84, 86, 89, 110, 116, 136, 142
Umar's Assurance of Safety, 5, 9, 12, 25, 55-56, 69, 75, 86, 102, 112, 114, 122, 142
Umayyads, 25
Usama Ibn Zaid, 45, 47, 48, 52

W

Al-Waqidi, 25, 47, 58, 60, 74

Y

Al-Ya'qubi, 57-60, 74, 82
Yazid Ibn Abi Habib, 68

Z

Zakat, 65
Zionists, 99

ISLAMICJERUSALEM STUDIES

- is a New Field of Inquiry, and a new branch of human knowledge based on interdisciplinary and multidisciplinary approaches to the study of the Islamicjerusalem region.
- was founded by Professor Abd al-Fattah El-Awaisi, a British Arab Historian, in the UK in 1994.
- is working towards educating the next generation of scholars, both nationally and internationally, and addressing the needs of our societies by investing in human capital through preparing and developing an international core academic team of young graduates, as specialists in the field, who meet the international standard.
- has published an academic referred journal *Journal of Islamicjerusalem Studies* in both English and Arabic languages, since 1997.
- holds an 'Annual International Academic Conference on Islamicjerusalem Studies' in the UK since 1997 (the forthcoming conference is the ninth conference which will be held on 1 June 2007).
- To institutionalise this new field in the UK:

  o the post of 'Chair in Islamicjerusalem Studies' was created in 2001.
  o the research centre 'Centre for Islamicjerusalem Studies' was established in 2002.
  o taught and research postgraduate programmes which lead to MLitt and PhD degrees from the University of Aberdeen were founded.
  o a number of research dissertations and theses have been written in the field (10 PhD theses and 24 dissertations) between 2002 and 2006.

- A number of monographs have been published in this field, including the groundbreaking monograph *Introducing Islamicjerusalem* which was launched in three countries: UAE at Zayed University on 25 December 2005, Scotland – UK at the Scottish Parliament in Edinburgh on 30 January 2006, and Qatar at Qatar University on 9 March 2006. In addition, it was translated and published in Arabic by Dar El-Fikr El-Arabi in Cairo in December 2006. It is also in the process of being translated and published (2007) in French and Malay.
- For a long time, the Founder has been adamant that 'the political agenda and its activisms and scholarship be separate.' He argues very strongly that 'political movements, religious or secular, in the Arab Muslim countries restrict the intellectual development of scholars and impose restrictions on their freedom of thought.' He also argues, 'To be taken seriously, any academic agenda should be taken away from religious or political agendas.' However, he encourages engagement and co-operation between "Knowledge and Power".

دراسات بيت المقدس
(الأحلام تتحول إلى حقائق)

- حقل معرفي أكاديمي جديد، وفرع جديد من المعرفة الإنسانية القائمة على منهجية الحقول المعرفية المتداخلة والمتعددة لدراسة إقليم بيت المقدس.

- تأسس عام 1994 في بريطانيا على يد المؤرخ الفلسطيني البروفيسور/ عبد الفتاح العويسي.

- يعمل على تشكيل وتخريج نواة من المختصين الأكاديميين المحترفين على المستوى الدولي، وتطوير قدرات وكفاءات أكاديمية على مستوى عالٍ.

- تصدر له مجلة أكاديمية محكمة باللغتين العربية والإنجليزية "مجلة دراسات بيت المقدس" منذ عام 1997.

- يعقد له "مؤتمر أكاديمي دولي سنوي" في بريطانيا منذ عام 1997 (المؤتمر القادم هو المؤتمر التاسع في 2007/6/1).

- استحدث لهذا الحقل المعرفي منصب "أستاذ كرسي لدراسات بيت المقدس" في بريطانيا عام 2001.

- أسس له مركز بحوث "مركز دراسات بيت المقدس" في بريطانيا عام 2002.

- أنشأ له برنامج تدريسي لمنح درجتي "الماجستير" و"الدكتوراة" في "دراسات بيت المقدس" من جامعة أبردين العريقة (الدراسة والبحث باللغة الإنجليزية فقط).

- كتب في موضوعاته عدداً من الأطروحات الأكاديمية باللغة الإنجليزية (10) رسائل دكتوراة، و(24) رسالة ماجستير.

- طبع في موضوعاته عدداً من الكتب الأكاديمية، يأتي في مقدمتها الكتاب الهام والمميز "تقديم بيت المقدس" للمؤرخ الفلسطيني البروفيسور/ عبد الفتاح العويسي الذي كتبه بداية باللغة الإنجليزية ونشره الناشر الأكاديمي لمعهد آل مكتوم في بريطانيا عام 2005، ثم ترجم إلى اللغة العربية ونشرته دار الفكر العربي بالقاهرة عام 2006، وترجم – كذلك – إلى اللغة الفرنسية والماليزية وسيتم نشرهما هذا العام (2007).

- يدعو المؤسس لهذا الحقل المعرفي – ومنذ عهد بعيد – إلى "ضرورة الفصل بين البرامج والنشاطات السياسية الحزبية وبين العمل البحثي الأكاديمي". ويؤكد بقوة أن "الحركات السياسية – سواء العلمانية أم الدينية – في الدول العربية والمسلمة تحد من التطور الفكري للعلماء، وتضع القيود على حريتهم الفكرية". ويحاجج بأنه "إذا أردنا أن نأخذ أية خطة عمل أكاديمية مأخذ الجد، فلابد من فصلها عن الإرتباطات السياسية الحزبية والتزاماتها". ويطالب بضرورة التواصل والتعاون بين "المعرفة والسلطة".